Confessions of an American None

A Credo of Sorts

Rachel Roberts, ThM

DEDICATION

*To all the Nones
who had the courage
to come out of the prayer closet.*

cre•do

/ krēdō, krādō/

noun

a statement of the beliefs or aims which guide someone's actions.

A credo is like a burrito—lots of stuff wrapped inside a simple package. Sometimes spicy.

CONTENTS

ACKNOWLEDGMENTS

My deepest gratitude to the innumerable persons I've known over the years, representing many different religions or no religion at all, who taught me that Love transcends labels.

For their investment of time, energy, and support during the writing of this book, I thank Steven Lindsey, Tabitha Bogard, Art Young, Denise Shaw, Emily Robnett, and Sebron Snyder.

For my mother who has taught me to feel and be sensitive, and my father who taught me to think and believe that I can do whatever I set my mind to, I am indebted.

My three children, Maxine, Major, and Merry, are constant sources of inspiration and motivation.

My family, I love you.

A CREDO OF NONE

Love is God.
People are mostly good.
Life is colorful, sometimes painful,
and always worth living.
I am my own worst enemy.
I recognize Love in myself and others.
We are One Human Family.
Love is my religion.

THE BREAKUP LETTER

It's not you. It's me.

I've searched my heart—mercilessly—and have put a ton of thought into this. The thing is, I've tried to adapt to you. To work with you. To sacrifice parts of myself so that we can stay together. But apparently, I'm just not capable of making it work.

You see, I don't know who you are anymore. We started out with the promise of love and commitment. I was eagerly optimistic. I deeply want to be loved and have an intimate relationship that makes me feel secure in this big bad world. I probably want that more than anything else in life.

But the promises you made devolved into controlling rules that left me with burdened sadness and isolation. You became territorial and were really judgmental of my friends. You shut me out when you disapprove of me or don't understand me. And sometimes there have been serious mind games. You try to convince me to believe a reality that, well, isn't real. Almost as crazy as saying the earth is flat! I'm embarrassed to be seen with you when you act this way. And in my experience, you are like this way more than you're not.

I can't be myself with you and you make me feel like shit.

On second thought, maybe it is you.

INTRODUCTION

Humans, We Have A Problem

The problems that I have wrestled with concerning religion seem to be ubiquitous in the Western 21st-century world. In the simplest of terms, religion appears to be less relevant to living.

Educated, self-aware, good folks can only offer a silent eye-roll when asked to believe outlandish doctrines that defy reason or science. The arrogance and exclusivity of certain religious groups seek to deprive the LGBTQ community and other marginalized groups of full human status, operating devoid of compassion and basic human decency. Religious practices, like attending church or reading the Bible, often do nothing to mitigate suffering and produce genuine happiness. And then there's always the issue of corruption, hypocrisy and abuse within the church.

Religion hasn't kept up with the times and the alternatives are equally left wanting. New Ageism commands similar fantastical beliefs and practices. Crystals, anyone? Mercury retrograde mean anything to you? The sterility of atheism is far from comforting to most. If your best friend suddenly gets hit by a Mack Truck, grief is not lessened by knowledge about the connection of emotional trauma and neurotransmitters, or awareness of the statistical probability of getting hit by a Mack Truck. Maybe some un-adulterated positive thinking, motivational Rah Rah is the answer. But after shelling out several hundred dollars to attend a cheerfest with 30,000 other people who paid the same, you are still left looking yourself in the mirror while the celebrity guru enjoys a vacay in Fiji.

Despite organized religion falling apart at the seams, the striving for connection to something greater than ourselves unwaveringly persists. This leaves many of us in a pickle because religion has been the one human institution that has made claims to satiate that longing of the human soul.

A None With New Habits

Most Christians would say that I'm not a Christian based on my position on many things critical to the dogma. Hardcore secularists would question why I give religion any merit whatsoever. For most of life, I have been trying to reconcile spiritual and religious leanings with being an intellectual, reason-based person living in a globally and digitally connected world. I have tried endless mental gymnastics to try and fit in the religious world and have tried to reason my way out of desiring a spiritual life. Neither has worked. My true nature is in a fluid space somewhere between.

Hence the rejection of labels, which makes me a None.

In my experience, most people really care about the deepest existential concerns of being human. But you'd hardly know that because we have been conditioned not to freely talk about these things. The only difference between me and scores of other people has been that I am obsessed with this pursuit and feel compelled to speak. Loudly.

This obsession led me to study the philosophy of religion in my undergraduate work and eventually to receive a Master of Theology degree from a progressive Methodist seminary. All this proves is that I am dedicated—not that I have all the answers. More important than any degree acquired has been the internal spiritual work that ironically transformed me into a None.

I Feel The Earth Move

While you are reading this, over 4,000 Americans are defecting from religious affiliation. This daily figure is derived from the landmark Pew Research Center report, *America's Changing Religious Landscape,* from 2015. Collectively, these folks are called Nones because they check the "none" box when asked to select their religion.

The unaffiliated have burgeoned to well over 90 million people today. Nones account for nearly 1 in 3 Americans, constituting the largest "religious" group in our country with only Evangelical Christianity narrowly behind.[i] At the current pace, our country is rapidly becoming a dominantly secular nation.

According to the *Religious Landscape* report, Nones should not be confused with atheists and agnostics, who account for about 6% of the total population combined. Rather, Nones are people who still recognize some sort of spirituality or belief in God but no longer identify with a particular religion. (Other reports include atheists and agnostics as a subset in the None category.) What Nones reject, more than anything, is not a concept of God or even the existence of religion— it is labels.

Pew provides additional evidence fortifying a bold new trajectory of America's spiritual climate. According to a 2018 Pew report, 61% of the American population range between being "solidly secular" to "relaxed religious." The latter demarcation reflects people who don't think religion is necessary for all people but may find personal value in it even though they rarely participate in traditional religious practices.

The trend is undeniable. The old way of being spiritual is on the way out.

The question becomes, *What, if anything, will replace it?* Nones are in the process of formulating that very answer.

What To Expect In This Book

St. Augustine of Hippo (354-430 CE) is heralded as one of the most influential Christian figures ever. He had lived a rather debaucherous life before converting to Christianity in his early 30s and going on to help shape the religion as we know it today through his writings and teachings. Sometime after his conversion, he wrote *Confessions* in which he penitently accounts for his life and transformation from hedonism to Christianity.

In this book I am using the word *confessions* in the theological sense. This basically means that I am confessing (or admitting) my statement of beliefs. Like Augustine of *his* time, I am departing from the norms of *my* time. Unlike Augustine, I am fleeing institutional Christianity rather than finding refuge in it.

My confessions are organized in the form of a credo, which is a formula of belief anchored by key topics. Each chapter in this book represent topics germane to my becoming a None. And along the way, we have some fun.

For example, each chapter contains references to recipes found in the Appendix and accompanying music that can be found on the official American None Spotify channel. Chapter One starts with dessert because, well, why not? (*Spoiler Alert* I will tell you upfront that one of the things I have most assuredly come to believe is that one can be deeply spiritual *and* have fun.)

A note about the paperback edition is required. The first publication of this book was in eBook form and included all kinds of fun hyperlinks that provided visual extrapolations on a theme or just sheer silliness. So if you want to read more about the Pando Aspen grove, hear the *Good Will Hunting* monologue, or groove to Mavis Staples, you'll have to do the googling yourself.

A Party Of None

I've been wanting to write this book for a few years but struggled because I love *everybody*. I haven't wanted to offend the rich diversity of people that I admire, appreciate and respect.

In both my personal relationships and through years of interfaith advocacy work, I've been friends and served along with people of countless different religions and worldviews. These include Methodism, Judaism, atheism, the B'hai faith, New Ageism, Catholicism, Mormonism, Sikhism, Hinduism, Islam, Native American traditions, Buddhism and many more. I have learned from all of them and am grateful to share this complex, deeply rewarding human experiment called life with them. While we may differ in expressions, my experience with diversity only strengthens my awareness of the Oneness of all human beings.

However, it is worth noting that this book is written for Nones by a None. I speak in an honest way meant to stoke a larger, transparent conversation *for the benefit of Nones*. While my views may differ from my religious friends, my love and appreciation for them does not waver.

I spent years of my life trying to force fit into a religious framework, went through a protracted period of denial, and finally found freedom in truth and Love independent of religious affiliation. Wherever a None may find her or himself on their journey, it is my hope that we may step out into our truth and community with one another. Knowingly or not, we are members of a cultural and spiritual revolution.

This is a wake-up call for religion and a rally cry for Nones— you are not alone.

CHAPTER 1

GOD

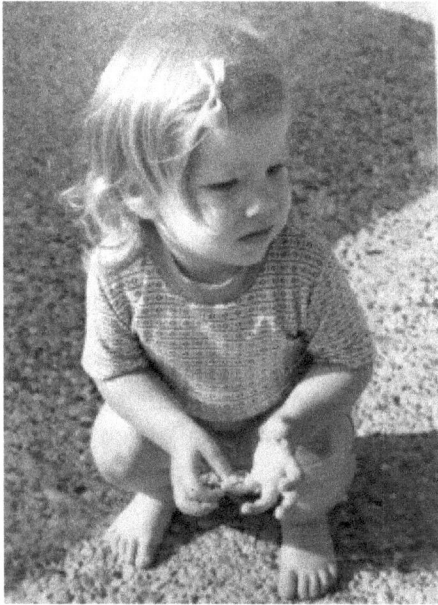

It seems I was born a deep thinker. Who knows what is going through my toddler mind here. Probably something like, *"How many licks* does *it take to get to the center of a Tootsie Pop?*

Opener: Do you pop out at parties? Are you unpoopular?

In 1952, Lucille Ball drank too much Vitameatavegamin and heralded the fate of my social life decades ahead of time. I was pretty "unpoopular" at parties.

One of my favorite sports, when I was in my mid-20s, was to shock people at parties. Not by siphoning beer from a keg but by demonstrating that I had a brain and was willing to talk about taboo subjects. I was a fitness instructor who wore lycra for a living and guys would assume I just liked to party and have pillow fights with my girlfriends while wearing nothing but bras and panties.

So imagine the surprise of my unsuspecting victim, when I would coolly weave the topic of religion into our small-talk conversation in just under two minutes. I was always bemused to watch some poor guy, who was just cruising for a good time, suddenly try to access the deeper files in his drunken brain so he could appear intelligent. Typically the guy would say he was a Christian but when pressed, he hadn't been to church since his mom quit making him go when he was a teen. And nine times out of 10, this party guy knew nothing about Christian doctrine or history. Yet he was willing to label his deepest sense of self as Christian.

Writhing out of the ontological snare I had laid, the guy would then try to turn the tables and ask me, "Do *you* believe in God?"

To which I would reply with a deadpan expression, "Define God and I'll tell you if I believe it."

Whomp, whomp, whomp.

Needless to say, nobody was getting laid.

Menu & Music: Miss American Pie

I begin with the subject of God because the concept of God is the lynchpin behind everything religious. It is kind of like your choice of fruit in a fruit pie.

Let's make an apple pie. (I mean, I am an *American* None, right?) The apple is not only the star ingredient of the pie but also generates the essence of the pie. Take away the apples and you are left with relatively bland ingredients like flour, butter, sugar, and cornstarch. What manifests the life and identity of the pie are the apples. Nobody ever says I just ate the best flour pie, even though flour is a primary ingredient.

Much in the same way, a religion's conception of God infuses everything else about that religion. This happens directly and indirectly. The Christian notion of the Trinity (God, Jesus, and Holy Spirit) is the hallmark theological differentiation from the other Abrahamic traditions- Judaism and Islam. This doctrinal banner would be like the decorative slice of apple placed on the top center of a baked pie for all to see.

On the other hand, the thick filling of the pie tastes like apple but didn't directly have any apple in it when placed in the oven. Rather, as the pie bakes, the juices of the apples mix with the other ingredients and voila!, an apple filling is created. This filling likens to the attitudes, mores, traditions, etc. of a religion that evolved over time and bind the community.

Let's dig in!

The Backstory: The Dude Abides

As a kid growing up in a fundamentalist loony bin, the existence of God was as obvious as white on rice. All rice comes in a box with a genteel looking African-American man on it and is always, always a sanitized white. Nobody questioned this. Ever.

In fact, anyone who would dare to question the existence of God, much less make the scandalous claim of atheism, was such an anathema that they were treated like *He Who Must Not Be Named* in Harry Potter.

God was everywhere. He saw everything, heard everything, directed everything. But He really liked hanging out in his house, which was an aluminum-sided building recessed on a piney woods lot. Betcha didn't know God had an actual street address.

My favorite time of the week was Sunday from about 9am until 12:30pm. We got to visit God at His place! These weekly outings were the closest thing to a flicker of light in an otherwise dark existence.

Going to church was the only time I was assured that my stepdad wouldn't beat me for a sin that God apparently told him that I had committed. Yeah, it's kinda twisted I know. God would rat on me and my stepdad would hunt me down with his belt and make mincemeat out of my back and legs.

But if I worshipped God fervently enough on Sunday mornings, maybe I could quit sinning so carelessly. Or maybe I could make God happy and He would give me a hall pass every now and then.

It may surprise you to know that the list of cardinal sins includes: failing to place the remote control on the left Lazy-Boy armrest, failing to close the iced tea pitcher with the slotted opening over the spout, or failing to have an I'm-just-fine-happy-but-actually-scared-out-of-my-mind look on my face in every waking moment. You would think that failing was the common sin here. But God is too enigmatic for such simplicity.

Case in point; when I repeatedly made "straight A's" several grading periods in a row, God told my stepdad that I was cheating the whole time. First I was beaten for "lying" when I denied cheating. Then I was beaten for the act of (allegedly) cheating. Remember, God is watching and He likes to keep you on your toes.

Our little merry band of ignoramuses would bolt from the real world and flock to the Home Depot church building—I'm sorry, God's House—like waterbugs fleeing the scene in search of darkness when the light turns on. Because "out there" in the big, bad, evil world, things were dirty. There were liberals and Catholics and Jews and dare I say, persons of a homosexual lifestyle. But when we collected at God's House, we were safe from all those monsters. We got to worship our God and reaffirm to one another how superior we were to the rest of humanity.

I left home at age 16 to go live with my atheist father. This ushered in a decade of agnosticism, in which I earnestly studied all major religions, various worldviews, and philosophies. I was on the hunt with a restless spirit.

I could never go so far as to consider myself an atheist. This was in part because the notion of God's existence had quite literally been beaten into me for nearly all of my life. Removing even the *possibility* of God would have been like trying to remove the mitochondria from my body. It (a sense of God) was just a pervasive part of me.

This pull toward connection with something transcendent eventually led me to a progressive, Methodist-founded seminary. I began in my late 20s only to have parenthood stall the plan. Later in my early 40s, I finally graduated with a Master of Theological Studies degree. Here I learned the complex and often sordid history of Christianity, the layers and uncertainties of the composition of the Bible, a kind and social justice version of Jesus, and that theologians were just as prone to be ego-driven as anyone. I was also exposed to the mystical tradition of Christianity which is obfuscated, in large measure, by the bombastic near-sightedness of Protestantism in our culture.

As enlightening as these discoveries were to me, it didn't stop me from taking a wild ride on the religious crazy train one more time. I had married and divorced my first husband (starter marriage, good guy, just not meant to be) and was a single mom with one child when I met Husband #2 (wait for it....) in church!

It was a conscious experiment on my part to visit this sprawling evangelical megachurch that was like an all-inclusive resort with religion sold as the main commodity, God as their CEO, and Jesus as their mascot. At the time the progressive, mainline Protestant churches I had previously attended had solid, inclusive theology but were arid and had virtually no support systems for marriages or single mothers. Enter "Megachurchland" that claimed to have answers to it all. I'll have more to say about this church experience later, but the immediately relevant thing is how God was used.

Husband #2 ended up being the kind of guy that provides the bulk of fodder for the Lifetime channel, scared the bejeezus out of Julia

Roberts or prompted J. Lo to take up Krav Maga. Megachurch-land's God would have an abused woman "go to her prayer closet" and pray for the abuser. This God commanded that an abused woman love by example, even when you are afraid he will kill you. And this God also endorses His followers to condemn a woman who finally leaves such a man.

Thus far, God had not been too keen on me my entire life. By the time I left my second husband, this time a single mother with three children, unemployed and landlocked in a city with no family or support system, I knew that either God had to change or I did. Or maybe it was both.

Confessions

Confession #1: God Evolves as Humans Do

More accurately put, our conception of God evolves to reflect our understanding of reality. The ancient Hebrews first worshipped multiple gods with various attributes associated with nature or the human condition as was the norm in the world at the time. God eventually consolidated into one being that reflected a sense of unified Israelite identity and nationalism. This God was still prone to rule like a human king, sometimes indulging in anger and revenge. (Wrong move and I will smite you!)

Jesus enters the picture and the Greco-Roman world was quick to merge bastions of Greek philosophy with emergent Christian theology wrapped in Roman customs. Following many internal fights, papal coups, and holy wars, Christianity lands with a thud on the American continents 1500 years later. After the self-righteous obliteration of indigenous cultures and religions and the splitting of Christian denominations ad infinitum, American Christianity now leads with a God that builds walls and bullies those who are different and oppressed while commanding that you worship Him. As I said, God reflects a people's conception of reality.

(For the record, the only time I ever reference God using a gender specific pronoun is when I am speaking within the context of a particular religion's conception that God indeed has a gender. I do not hold this belief myself.)

The study of history compiled by legitimate scholars renders the evolution of the human conception of God as a fact. Not to mention that basic common sense informs us that there are countless versions of "God" currently in the world spanning religions, denominations, cultures, and individuals.

A modern-day, praise-band, donut-eating, name-it-and-claim-it type of Christian today wouldn't even recognize the God of the ancient desert monks in early Christendom. This early Christian God of the monastic traditions evoked an ascetic lifestyle whose adherents routinely deprived themselves of food and sleep and prayed non-stop every day often with some form of self-mutilation in place. Imagine the full body shock a contemporary churchgoer would have, mouth agape and donut in hand, if he were transported back in time to the caves of the Nitrian desert in Egypt. The stone washed jeans and ironic beard would suddenly seem gratuitous and anachronistic.

You can also simply evaluate your own conception of God and how it has evolved over the course of your life. Chances are your God has also morphed if you are willing to take a critical look at it. And if your God hasn't evolved, then it is probably time to check under the hood and see how things are working. For me God began as a megalomaniac, fire-breathing sadist. Then there was no God but faint intellectual abstractions for about 10 years. Next the Supreme Sadist reappeared, and finally I redefined all of it, which I will get to later.

Confession #2: God Did Not Make Your Football Team Win

Or provide that front-row parking spot when you were in a hurry at Target. Skill, preparation, and sometimes even luck wins football games. Chance or a keen eye secures open parking places.

Need I say more?

Confession #3: God Does Not Have a Plan for Your Life

There is this common theme in American Christianity that God has some divine plan for your life, only he won't tell you what it is, which leaves you constantly fretting over whether or not you are living according to the plan. This neurosis beleaguers many well-intentioned people who genuinely desire to live a noble, spiritual life. But "God's Plan" is also hearkened by many more folks who use the idea to explain away the unexplainable or justify their own importance.

Laments:
"My young child died of a rare form of cancer."
"My husband ran off with a sophomore in college and left me homeless."
"I will probably be evicted from my apartment despite working three jobs. I can't afford to live."

Answer: "God has a plan. Just trust him."

Translation: "I have no freakin' clue why such shitty things happen but I have to say something that sounds good."

When I used to believe that God had some undisclosed plan for my life, I was left to conclude that a life of abuse was the plan. I went to great lengths to make sense of that notion. Maybe God was refining me and fortifying my character or maybe I was so sinful and depraved that I deserved this hell on earth. I ultimately rejected both of those suppositions.

Many Christians will admit that God does not make bad things happen but this sticks in the craw of other Christians because that implies that Satan (God's Opponent Extraordinaire) has equal or greater power than God. So these Christians gerrymander their theology to say that God *allows* bad things to happen, usually for purposes that are too mysterious for us to be able to comprehend.

There's also a logic problem here. Check out this scenario. A man loses his entire family—a wife and two children—to a drunk driving accident. The surviving husband and father takes years to rebound emotionally and psychologically from this senseless loss. Eventually, he begins volunteer work to help other victims of drunk driving. This helps him heal and make sense of his own pain. It is common for an outsider, or maybe even the man himself, to say that the accident happened for the purpose that he could help subsequent victims in the same situation.

This is circular logic. If God had the power and authority to make or allow the drunk driving accident to happen so that the man could eventually help other drunk driving victims, why not just eradicate drunk driving or drunkenness in the first place? Get rid of the root problem instead of managing the symptoms. For that matter, the real root problem would be the inherent malaise, discontentment or vacuum that drives people to chronic drunkenness in the first place, which purportedly is what God is heralded to absolve. This logic train just did two circles around itself.

The idea of God's Plan can also reinforce a fragile ego's justification of its own importance. I've seen this happen frequently in churchy situations, including by yours truly.

Once a long time ago, a married couple came to me in tears because the husband had been diagnosed with prostate cancer and they were both scared. They knew I was in seminary and must have presumed I had the wisdom or maturity to comfort them. Some of the deadest words to ever come out of my mouth were to that sweet, anguished couple. Be strong, God has a plan, etc. I was sick on the inside because it felt as hollow as it must have sounded. But at the time, I quite simply didn't know what else to say.

Many years later, as a barely surviving single mom of three, I volunteered to lead a small women's church group that met weekly for spiritual study. I was still internally discombobulated by my second divorce. I believed that God had put me through all of that hell so that I could turn around and "help" other women. I put "help" in quotes because, as it turns out, my motives weren't clean.

Part of the process for leading this group was, over the course of a few weeks, each woman had to share her life story. In a gallant display of false humility, I signed up to be the very last person to share my story. I allowed all the other women to share their stories first so that I could join in the group sympathy for expressed woes and hardships and offer obligatory encouragement and positive affirmations afterward.

As the weeks wore on and I had yet to tell my story, what became glaringly apparent to me was that I was thinking in the background, *These chicks are going to be blown away by how much more difficult my life has been than theirs. They will be so impressed with how spiritual and kind I am considering the crap I've dealt with. These ladies really need me,* I would say to myself self-deferentially.

While I had entered this small group scenario believing that God had some plan that required this duty of mine, I left realizing that what I really wanted out of it was a sense of purpose and importance and maybe some sympathy. What's really telling is that I can barely remember anything about any of the other women in that group—that is how self-absorbed I was. My motives had been self-serving and disingenuous. That hard realization leveled me with true humility.

Confession #4: God is a Metaphor

Have you ever heard that Eskimos have over a hundred different words for snow? This is often said to espouse the notion that a language both affects and reflects a person's experience of reality. In this case, the casual thought is that Eskimos deal with snow in so many forms all the darned time that their orientation to life is essentially enmeshed with it. (Snow kabobs, grilled snow, baked snow, fried snow, snow salad, snow and potatoes...) The prominence of snow in their lives warrants the minute detail of language needed to speak about it *and conversely,* the nuanced language about snow heightens the Eskimos' perception and acumen about it.

I hate to burst your bubble but this cliché about the number of Eskimo words for snow is widely disputed by modern linguistic scholars. There are difficulties in defining the label Eskimo and in defining the meaning of "word" or "word roots" when tracing the etymology of both snow and Eskimo. Not to mention that the term Eskimo itself is pejorative to many of the various indigenous groups of people who have been lumped under this moniker by Westerners for hundreds of years. The preferred term, at least by many, is Inuit and refers to the native people of Alaska, Siberia, Canada, Greenland and other circumpolar regions of the North Pole.

Language is a metaphor of our thoughts, feelings, experiences, and perceptions of reality. If you don't believe me, just think back to the last time you and your significant other had an icky episode. Chances are one of you communicated "A" while the other person heard "B" and relationship mayhem ensued. And if you were the speaker, you thought to yourself, if he could just be in my heart or my mind, he would know that I did not mean it the way that he heard it. And he probably thought, if she really knew me then she wouldn't have said what she said!

Things often get lost in translation, whether it's due to the speaker, the listener or merely the inherent limitations of language. Unfortunately for us humans, we do not have Vulcan capabilities and mind melds are not possible. Language is the carrier of the internal reality that we are seeking to share with others. The Eskimo example illustrates the layers upon layers of complexities within language.

When I say God is a metaphor, I mean it in two ways. The word God in and of itself is a metaphor. The word is a symbol of what an individual, group, or religion means by the idea of God. This is why I could have so much fun at parties in my 20s and still feel a sense of correctness. I was basically asking the poor guy, "What is the meaning of your symbol vis-à-vis the word God?"

However, much hardship and many years later, I have come to understand God as a metaphor in a much deeper way. As touched upon previously, God has metamorphosed throughout history with changing attributes, personalities, powers, and abilities. From the Judeo-Christian perspective, this God is commonly viewed as an external being somewhere "out there" who is most certainly male. (Does the image of an old man with long white hair and a beard, wearing flowing white robes and sitting on a throne that is magically suspended by clouds seem familiar to you?) This is the same God who has secret plans, arbitrarily decides people's fates, wins football games, and likes bumper stickers with His name on it.

What I came to realize is that even *the way* we characterize God is a metaphor for our deepest, most existential yearnings or experiences. When we think of God as an old dude out there somewhere who, if we do the right things or believe the right things, will make life better for us, then that is a reflection of the interior mechanism we employ to navigate the difficulties of life. Something external, some self-contained being that I am not capable of understanding is supposed to come to my rescue.

This external-otherness notion of God is definitely what I believed for many years outside of my agnostic phase. That all came to a cataclysmic implosion during a moment that I consider to be the dawn of my spiritual awakening.

The Rosedale Experience

Imagine standing in your living room casually holding a telescope. In this scenario, your body is a participant in your normal reality. Everything is scaled relative to you. Your surroundings make physical and spatial sense. You can move about this world with ease because it is comfortable and familiar. For the sake of illustration, consider yourself in the neutral position here holding the telescope.

When you look through the telescope toward the night sky, you see a vast universe that renders yourself infinitesimally small, underscoring the question of your personal relevance on the planet. Suddenly you are a speck of dust upon dust holding your microcosmic telescope. It is like your very being instantaneously shrunk to amoebic size. You are no longer in a neutral position. You are now in the negative to the greatest degree.

Now imagine placing your eye against the large lens of a telescope and peering through the barrel toward the small end. Everything becomes a pinpoint reduced to minuscule scale, as if you are the Michelin Man hot air balloon looming imposingly over a miniature world. In this position, you are in the extreme positive to the greatest degree.

This is what it was like when the greatest pretense of my life shattered—the moment I realized there was no God "out there" that would one day deign to save me from my suffering. All the false constructs I had previously assumed in my life were instantaneously reduced to insignificance. My consciousness became a disoriented, infinite lummox hovering over my suddenly nano-sized world.

This experience took place when I was about 40 years old. I was leasing a tiny home built in 1922 on Rosedale Avenue. This was the first home post second divorce for my three children and me. I was unemployed, desperate for work, and finishing my master's degree. I was free from the abusive marriage but now assumed an entirely different set of unfathomable stresses.

Husband #2 was gallivanting around with his fourth wife who was nearly 30 years his junior. In fact, she was a sophomore in college when he first seduced her.

Meanwhile, I lived in daily, strangulating fear. I couldn't pay my bills, my bank account often had a negative balance, and I was fielding those incessant, nasty robocalls from scammers who prey on people in financial straits. Two of my children frequently had catastrophic meltdowns, the cat was peeing in the house, and I had no close friends or family nearby. Depending on what state my ex-husband was in, I was afraid he would kill my children in a drunk driving accident or show up and kill us all in our sleep.

The only thing that had carried me through life at this juncture had been the belief— the hope—that God would someday choose to relieve me of the oppressive darkness that seemed to follow me around. I had tried every Christian trick-of-the-trade: pray more, pray differently, pray out loud, pray silently, read the Bible, read it more, read it differently, be kind, be kinder, go to church, go more often, and so on. This was a lifetime accumulation of striving that hinged on the belief of a Rescue God.

It was an autumn evening and my kids were playing (or more likely fighting) in the next room. I was studying for one of my graduate classes at my desk in the back bedroom. The subject was the mystical traditions of ancient and modern-day contemplatives in both Christianity and Buddhism. I had come to observe that while there are definitely differences, there are overwhelming similarities when you sift out the fundamental tenets, the chief one was that the concept of God is *being itself* (verb) not *a* being (noun).[ii]

It was hard to concentrate on school work. A stressful thought turned into a tear. A tear turned into a monsoon. The crying became inconsolable. *Why wouldn't God relieve my burdens?* I was so alone and felt so desperate.

Suddenly the fabric of my consciousness violently ripped from top to bottom exposing a raw truth. There was NO God that would someday arrive. NO God that would someday sprinkle fairy dust and make things better. NO God that had been watching me from above. In short, my epiphany was that there was *nothing* out there.

When this hit me like a celestial hammer to the head, my mind became one with the side of the universe on the large end of the telescope. I was looking at my life on earth like it was teeny, tiny small. I felt all kinds of things but primarily I felt foolish. I had been *Waiting for Godot* for 40 years!

I rolled around erupting with tears beating my bed and screaming into the pillows, *There is NOTHING!!!!* I couldn't be mad at God because the God that I used to think I knew didn't exist. And I couldn't really be mad at anyone else because they were just perpetuating the pretense they had inherited. If anything, I felt like I had been the victim of some kind of generic cosmic joke but I wasn't sure who was laughing.

This internal reckoning was akin to a child discovering Santa isn't real or going through your first teenage breakup and realizing that your 16-year-old boyfriend didn't really love you and had been making out with your BFF behind your back. I was in an existential coma for several weeks following this experience. Once your consciousness squarely faces the truth about something, there is no going back.

What died for me during "The Rosedale Experience" was a false construct of God—the external-otherness of a personified masculine God who demotes humanity to sycophants en masse. This common Western Christian notion of God has produced humans like chickens who are bred in overcrowded conditions, never seeing the light of day, and not having the leg strength to stand on their own because they are passive recipients of burn 'em and churn 'em production. Ironically, this kind of God emasculates persons from their own accountability and yields self-indulgent thinking and behaviors.

Previously unbeknownst to me, I had bought into a God that was a metaphor for what I deeply desired: something/someone out there who would come rescue me and make me happy. The death of this God was the greatest gift I've ever received.

Confession #5: Your Greatest Super Power

My first three confessions told you what I think God is not. And the understanding of God as a metaphor segues the conversation into what I have come to believe that God is.

I now know God to be the Source of regenerative power that is available to me and everyone else on this planet. This is the power that allows you to see things from the side of the large lens of the telescope. It is not that your life becomes insignificant. Rather, your life is seen in the context of the Greater Whole. This in turn unleashes the Life Force, which is the power of *being itself* and is also Love, that maximizes your own individual life.

I say this all from experience. My mind, based on life experience, told me that I had nothing to live for during my darkest seasons. It was my very stark reality. But I used reason to surmise that history accounts for people, past and present, who have overcome greater odds than I had and they found peace and happiness.

Next, I stepped out in faith that life could be different and better. It is in the space between reason and faith where I believe the power that I call God activated and ushered me into a new way of being. For the first time in my life, as a forty-year-old woman, I knew that I was Loved and that I have the capacity to Love all people as part of our One Human Family.

Western Christianity has commonly characterized this power as an anthropomorphic God and science has sought to trace its origins to the biochemicals in the brain. These two disciplines can duke it out all they want but here is what I know: Religion and science ultimately seek to uncover the same truth: Ultimate Reality. I can't buy into the superfluous, antiquated trappings of worshipping a contrived personification of God. Nor does the knowledge of biochemicals assist me when I am entrapped by the conundrums of being human.

There are vastly more educated people than me in both disciplines who can articulate their arguments. It may be that one day scientists discover the origin of such power in the neurology of our brains. It may be that this power is sourced from another dimension of the universe that humans have yet to identify. In the meantime, I have become content not needing to know exactly where this Source originates. But I do know that it exists and works when one yields to it.

Confession #6: God is "Both/And"

One of life's greatest epiphanies for me centers around deodorant. Yes friends, deodorant.

I was a sophomore in college and taught several aerobics classes a week (think neon pink unitard, scrunchie socks, and white Reeboks). One evening while hanging with my dorm roommate and a pint of Cherry Garcia, she kindly but bravely told me that I stunk. Not only that, she admitted that I had a stinky *problem.*

I told her that I didn't understand how that could be the case. After all, I showered regularly and put on deodorant every morning.

To which she said, "Maybe you should put deodorant on at night, too."

I countered, "But you're supposed to put it on once a day in the morning." And upon further reflection added, "Maybe I have a body problem," feeling instant shame.

She said, "Rachel, you can put deodorant on more than once a day."

The heavens parted and the angels sang! Rose petals showered from the sky. Lavender sprang forth from our carpet. My roommate sang praises to the olfactory gods when she saw the dawn of realization spread across my face as her words of truth sank in. I walked into the bathroom and felt the liberation of applying deodorant *in the evening.* "Wow," I thought incredulously, "this *can* be done!"

What changed for me that evening (other than better personal hygiene practices) was the awareness of Do's vs. Do Nots, Is vs. Is Nots, Yes vs. No, Black vs. White. My mother had taught me to apply deodorant once a day in the morning when I was 10. I'm sure my prepubescent self didn't warrant more than that. But what remained in my mind for years was, you DO put deodorant on in the morning; you do NOT put it on any other time. That is called stinkin' thinkin'!

It is also called binary thinking. This oppositional way of viewing things by definition is limiting yet all too common. Initially, it serves practical purposes like teaching toddlers how to navigate the world. Milk = good. Bourbon = bad. Raw carrots = good. Snickers = bad. But as they grow older the conversation should evolve to include the nuance of moderation and context.

I have always been reticent about applying labels to myself. But I'm a hypocrite because the truth is, as humans, we are always labeling each other in order to expeditiously plow through life. We usually don't take the time to deep dive into a person, issue or situation to understand the nuances, gray areas, and tensions that exist. Categorical, binary thinking undergirds this tendency. It is a rightful, necessary mental mechanism when judiciously applied for the purposes of maintaining momentum in daily living.

As previously mentioned, the notion of God that I reject is one that personifies God with human attributes, which is typically an outcropping of binary thinking. But when God is understood as a Force, a Power, an unquantifiable Source, then articulating God's attributes requires greater sophistication.

The study of mystical Christianity, philosophical Buddhism and Taoism elevated my awareness of such a way of thinking. It is best described as "Both/And" thinking and is quintessential in my understanding of God as Love. Let me unpack what this means by describing the attributes of God that make sense to me.

God is both within and without.
It has become commonplace for American Christianity to extol the external otherness of God, which I have previously discussed. This characterization is attached to anthropomorphic constructs of God. This is primarily because to say that God is first and foremostly inside of you teeters on humanistic anathema in the

view of such Christians. Because, they say, if God is within you, then you are claiming to be God. Well, guess who also claimed to be one with God? Uh yeah, that guy named Jesus.

How and why humans ended up turning Jesus into being synonymous with God is an issue I take up later in the chapter on Beliefs. I, along with a minority of Christian mystics, believe that the message Jesus intended to impart to people is that the Love and Power of God is within each and every person. My favorite interpretation of Jesus' birth narrative, from divine conception through the nativity, also bolsters this claim. Essentially it is an etiological story that archetypally pronounces that divinity is intrinsic to every living person. As Lady Gaga sang, "We are born this way, baby!"

However, the God that is inherently within us all is also greater than us and external to us at the same time because this is the Source of Life, the Power that Transforms, and the Unity that Binds. The best analogy, although limited, is water. Our bodies are about 60 percent composed of water. This water permeates our entire being, present in our tissues, organs and blood cells. Water is also in the air we breathe. (Trust me, being from the South, I know ALL about humidity.) Water falls from the sky and of course, there are the obvious bodies of water that comprise rivers, lakes, oceans, icebergs and snow drifts. Water is both within and without us. Water is the source of life and the binding agent of all living things. It is virtually impossible to say where water begins or ends. It exists in both the DNA of us humans and the DNA structure of the universe. I think of God the same way.

One of my favorite Rumi quotes is, "You are not a drop in the ocean. You are the entire ocean in one drop." Sums it up!

God is both personal and impersonal.
In my mid to late 20s, I began the study of Tai Chi after having met a world-renowned Tai Chi master at an international fitness conference. I had the privilege of studying under him for a period of time. Since Tai Chi is considered moving meditation and is attributed to ancient Taoist monks, our conversations often veered into the arena of spirituality.

At this point in my life, I had recently emerged out of my agnostic phase and was finding newfound enthusiasm for the progressive theology of contemporary Methodism. My Tai Chi teacher and I were discussing the concept of God and met an interesting sticking point. I was claiming a personal relationship with God and my teacher said to me, somewhat baffled, *"I will never understand why some people feel it necessary to believe in a personal God."* To which I thought, *"What is the point of believing in God if God is not personal?"*

I now see it both ways.

God is impersonal in the sense that God is otherness that is greater than me and my ability to comprehend God's Godness as the Force, Source and Unity of all things good, right, and life-affirming. This is the part of me that recognizes the microbic scale of my life on the small end of the telescope while peering into the vast inexplicable nature of Ultimate Reality on the other side.

God is personal in the sense that God is part of my existential DNA. As an individual member of a sentient species, I have the ability to live in awareness and harmony with God or to remain mired in the trappings of my egoistic mind that thwarts unity with God. Essentially, I have the ability to have a relationship with this Force, Source and Unity. Or not. This is living in the clarity of awareness on the side of the large lens of the telescope, whereby your life on earth is not insignificant but scaled to the Whole. There is peace in this place.

God is both nothing and everything.
I have always enjoyed reading books about physics for dummies. My ability to fully understand and retain the complexities of this discipline is woefully deficient. I just stand on the sidelines, popcorn in hand, and marvel at the people in the big leagues as I try to follow the game. The single greatest fascination for me is the idea that you can divide matter infinitely, ultimately tracing our living reality to a tangible nothingness. And yet, here is life in all its grandeur!

The Rosedale Experience jarred me into "seeing" the nothingness of God. God is intangible and beyond concrete ascriptions or being. What I didn't tell you earlier is that my old way of thinking (mind attached to ego) is what went out kicking and screaming at this realization. The hovering lummox that had felt foolish and angry was my finite mind that had previously bought into a categorical God. This part of me took some time to fully recede. What replaced it though was well worth the growing pains.

My mind attached to ego was replaced by a vivid, expansive clarity of consciousness that saw the Whole of existence, the inter-connection of all things. This illuminated that God is everything. The torment and pain of life as a struggling, single mother of three ceased to feel like a personal affront. Rather, I saw the struggle as a part of the grander nature of life, not as an adversary.

In short, I was freed to accept reality while tapping into the Source, Force, and Unity of God to change myself from the inside out, which ultimately led to a change in my reality. Funny how things work!

Confession #7: God Unites Us

To say that God unites people probably flies in your face right now. All around us we see how God is used to divide people. The most extreme examples of this would be the Christian Crusades from nearly a millennia ago and modern Islamic terrorist activity today.

This division manifests in much smaller ways, of course, like the way I was taught to hold people of different ideologies in contempt when I was a child. Or how some churches ostracize people who are gay. Or the group of stay-at-home, Bible-study soccer moms who ignore the refugee family from Syria in their social activities. The God that is used to cause divisions such as these is the categorical, anthropomorphic, tribal God that ego-driven human minds create.

When I say that God unites us, I am referring to God that is the Power beyond what is apparent to us, the Both/And that transcends categories and the Presence awash in all things. Humans do not always live with this awareness, thereby creating massive waves of destruction at times, but it does not make it any less true.

The Source of Love is what I call God. I firmly believe that a kind, loving devout Christian and a kind, loving atheist mathematician both seek the same thing—a sense of place and purpose on this earth. The Christian uses the word God. The mathematician rejects the word God. But both seek ultimate truth. They just have different languages and practices used to explore that truth that gives them their sense of place and purpose.

Persons living a life of humility and Love may experience God in different ways, through sports, nature, science, philanthropic work, the arts, academia, craftsmanship, the list is endless. Whatever endeavor that connects people to one another and to the vibrancy of living is the carrier for the binding agent that I believe is meant by the term God.

The Dovetail: Parting Thoughts, Summations, and a Send-Off

A Rose Is Still a Rose...

One of the most famous vignettes of Shakespeare is the balcony scene where Juliet bewails that her love Romeo is ostracized simply because his name belongs to a rival family. She decries,

> *What's in a name? that which we call a rose*
> *By any other name would smell as sweet;*
> *So Romeo would, were he not Romeo call'd,*
> *Retain that dear perfection which he owes*
> *Without that title. (2.2.45-49)*

Romeo remains Romeo, with all of his enduring attributes, regardless of his name. The name itself does not make the man. Similarly, just because a person says that they believe in or know God, does not mean that they do. And just because a person says that they do not believe in God, does not mean that they don't know God.

The God of my present understanding—Source and Power of Love—has always been and will always be. This reality withstands the convolutions and baggage that humans have attached to the name throughout history. Love unites us regardless of how we identify God.

Sometimes, I use the words Love (capitalized) and God interchangeably. I choose the term that will resonate best with my present company. If I'm talking to a senior adult at a retirement home, I will refer to God. If I am speaking with someone who is disenchanted with religion, I will refer to Love. The underlying message remains the same. I'm simply choosing my linguistic metaphors according to the listener.

As a None, my personal preference is to use the term Love as the utmost expression of what is commonly meant by the word God. There is only One Love yet humans have created many Gods. Further, Love is a verb, which more accurately depicts my understanding of God. And God, at least in the English language, is strictly confined to a noun, which is terribly problematic as I've delineated in this chapter. Ultimately though, our words mean far less than our actions.

On Parking Spaces, Football Games and Divine Plans

When I happen upon front-row parking or succeed at an endeavor (my version of winning a football game), I have come to receive it solely through the lens of gratitude and prompt me to make the world a better place for other people.

Life can be challenging on its own terms. So when little things like convenient parking happens, I am reminded to step up my game looking for ways to spread happiness in other people's lives. Even small gestures like making eye contact with a cashier and asking about their day can serve to pivot that person's outlook for the day. Never underestimate small acts of kindness.

On a larger scale, experiencing success reminds me that we rise (and fall) together. Nothing notable happens without the efforts or influences of many people. Therefore, when I succeed in some way, rather than viewing it as a reflection of me, I see the reflection of others. This in turn propels me to empower others toward their own versions of success.

Regarding God's plan for my life, I recognize only one plan for my life, which I happen to believe is the plan for all people. I am to live a life fueled by and manifested by Love. It's really that simple. I am more concerned about why and how I do something than the outcome. I believe that if I am centered in Love, the proper outcomes will take care of themselves.

In practical terms, we all have gifts and talents unique to us. It is our job to be good stewards of those gifts and talents, including doing our best to make sound decisions. In the end, life has twists and turns often that are unpredictable. We must let go of the outcomes and keep our primary purpose centered on the infinite goal of Love.

I'm More Fun at Parties Now!

Changing God changed my life.

Remember that apple pie we made together? The selection of apple as the fruit flavored the entire pie. How we conceive of God flavors how we understand and experience critical facets of life, including pain and suffering, success and failure, and how we value our world and ourselves.

When I changed the way I understood God, all these other facets of life improved exponentially for me. I shed the external otherness, anthropomorphic male deity God and embraced a God that is Source, Force, and Unity of Love—a God that dwells inexplicably within and without, who is personal yet infinitely greater than any one person, who is everything Life-Affirming and yet mysteriously nothing tangible. *This God* resurrected me from living death.

I discovered my greatest happiness and infinite freedom while still in the most harrowing of circumstances. I was transformed from the inside out by Love as God. This unleashed me to fully love myself and others and actualize my full potential, a charge that is a gift-in-waiting for all people.

So in the spirit of Kansas (the band, not the state), let's "Carry On" toward the subject of Humanity and the World.

CHAPTER 2

HUMANITY & THE WORLD

Behind the levee at my grandparent's place was a dammed tributary of the Red River where we often went fishing.

Opener: Hook, Line, and Sinker

Worms.

I used to go cane pole fishing with my grandmother on my grandparents' lake. But I had a problem. I was deathly afraid to bait the hook. I don't know if it was the wiggliness of the worms or the actual piercing of their gelatinous bodies that bothered me most. I wanted to make my grandmother proud but couldn't bring myself to commit wormicide.

Every time... *every* time she would hook the worm for me and assuage my conflicted emotions. We would then sit with our lines in the water and just be together. And on a rare occasion, I would catch a little bream and how we would both delight in the marvel of it all.

She was a true Southerner who had the imprint of aristocracy with the no-nonsense ethos of a pioneer. Almost parallel to Scarlett O'Hara, her family lost its amassed wealth in the Great Depression and she was forced to recalibrate to the reality of scarcity.

Her life took a material turn upward throughout her 70-year marriage to my grandfather, who rose from being dirt-poor to a successful oil man. But this didn't change her ethic. She was never impressed with material things, loved Jesus so much that my grandfather should have been jealous, and spent a lifetime extending care and attention to many of the poorest children in our hometown.

Another thing that never changed about my grandmother was her Louisianian drawl. We didn't open windows. We opened *windahs*. We didn't drink water. We drank *whorter*. My grandfather wasn't in the oil business. He was in the *awl* business. No one ever had an idea. We had *idears*.

One time over lunch, my grandmother earnestly asked my brother, "Paaaaaawl, do you like jala*penis*??" Uproarious laughter ensued.

My grandmother made me feel loved. She was a teacher and inspired me to be the same. She taught me to marvel at nature and to care for those who are hurting. I cannot imagine how bleak my life would have been without her.

Oh, there is one more thing she had in common with Scarlett O'Hara.

She was racist.

Menu and Music: Everyday People

You probably grew up like me being taught that America was a melting pot of people and cultures. In recent years that metaphor has been panned due to its colonialistic inferences. A more common metaphor these days is that America is like a salad. Different types of people from different cultures all tossed together with the American identity like the dressing that envelopes us all.

So it seemed fitting to assign a salad to the chapter on Humanity. My recipe for *Eclectic Salad* is sure to inspire your imagination and delight your taste buds.

The Backstory: Deep in the Heart of Duplicity

If religion was like mud in your veins in late 20th century Louisiana, racism was the coronary heart disease. I had no appreciation at the time but my generation straddled the remnants of one era and the painful birth of another.

Like many cultural waves that are slow to gain traction in the south, desegregation in public schools had a very slow start in Shreveport. By the time I began elementary school in the late '70s, busing had finally become normative. I was a little kid with virtually zero awareness of the horrific history of institutionalized racism and bigotry that founded our nation. And I was entirely ignorant of the grave fight that was currently underway for human equality.

At the time, all I knew was that my two best friends were Vizita and Tara. I never even thought about the fact that their skin was darker than mine—until Tara and I wanted to play together after school and it was treated like some forbidden request. Only once did I go to Tara's house and she came to mine. The unspoken feeling was that we were breaking some sort of law by going into each other's neighborhoods. I remember Tara's mother being a beautiful, gracious single mom. I can only speculate that it was racist fear that prevented my parents from letting me see Tara more.

Not only were there leftover attitudes and mores from the antebellum south in my hometown, there were also tangible cues that our culture was still steeped in racism over one hundred years after the civil war.

Before my mother married my step father, she was an industrious single mom herself. As a reprieve to her hard-working life, she would drive my little brother and me out to visit my grandparents who had several acres south of town. In order to get there, we had to cut through hundreds of acres of cotton fields. My mother's little butterscotch Nissan zipped along the country road as I watched the rows of southern snow whip by me at a dizzying speed. Cotton as far as the eye could see in any direction.

The physical beauty of this sight was ominously undermined by what it represented. Shanties punctured the landscape as a stark reminder of generations of labor force who used to work those fields. Even when I was a child, there were still some families living in these tiny, thin-walled cabins that looked like they would collapse with the slightest gust of wind.

By contrast, my grandparents' sprawling estate included pasture land with cattle, barns, a workshop for my grandfather, and a levee with a lake and tennis court on the other side. My grandmother had a tiny "museum" where she collected bird and wasp nests, insects and butterflies (who had met their demise naturally), snake skins, and other curiosities. The main house hearkened a plantation home with its pale yellow hue, white columns and green shutters. A miniature version served as a playhouse for us kiddos. The shiny tar driveway ran parallel to rows of pecan trees, remnants from a former orchard.

When our little car approached, my grandmother would be waiting for us at the end of the driveway, smiling radiantly and waving enthusiastically.

My brother and I would amuse ourselves by seeing who could go the highest in the tire swing that hung from a giant Southern oak tree. We climbed the hay bales in the barn and hoped we'd never see a mouse or a snake. We chased each other around a fig tree that had a girth wide enough to win a prize at the state fair if there were a contest for such a thing. Granddaddy's beehives were often buzzing with activity, a signal to stay away. So we would redirect and ride our Big Wheels down the side of the levee and then go pick wild blackberries. If we were feeling brave enough, we'd visit the family pet cemetery up on a little hill and pretend we weren't spooked. The sound of my grandmother clanging a giant cast iron bell would momentarily freeze us in our places and then we would head back over the levee for some of her mediocre cooking.

Unless it was Eloise who had done the cooking. Eloise was a maid who worked for my grandmother for decades and we quietly admitted she was a much better cook. My grandfather employed a man named Beau who did manual labor for him for nearly the same duration of time. Eloise and Beau seemed like a part of the fabric of our family. I don't know if they felt the same way though. That was easy for us to say because they were making our lives easier but they had to return to their own lives, which I can only imagine included much hardship.

I never had race relations conversations with my grandfather but my grandmother definitely made her views known. She was the kind of Southern woman who considered herself evolved on the issue but that wasn't saying much because the bar was abysmally low. I'm certain she would not have thought of herself as racist. She would have denounced the KKK and similarly related hate-based behaviors.

Rather, my grandmother exhibited latent racism that came in the forms of attitudes and beliefs. She would communicate things to me that suggested that *some* black people were good people. Or that "he was nice, even though he was black." She used the Bible to somehow corroborate her belief that black and white people are not meant to live next to one another, much less marry one another. And I remember picking up on the idea that if we (white people) did something nice for them (black people), it was a huge act of generosity on our part and they should be really grateful.

My southern childhood was replete with racist children's songs, jokes and antics. It was as if it was the "OK-not-OK" thing to joke about. I had dolls and books that were caricatures of African-American slaves. When I was a young girl, I used to play dress up in my grandmother's attic. She had some costume makeup and one time I darkened my skin and dressed like a maid to everyone's rapt amusement. None of this was ever called out as being racist.

The jarring paradox is that at school many of my best friends were African-American but at home, they became "the other" or "those people" as evidenced by the attitudes of my family. Living in this duality was normal to me. The gravity of this grievously errant cultural duplicity from my childhood sickens me to this day.

Quiet racism is still racism. It is based on fear and ignorance. In essence, it pits one group against another. It divides, not unites. It deals death, not life. There is no Love in racism.

I started this chapter with a story about my grandmother and how she was the greatest source of safety and love that I felt as a young girl. I also exposed the raw truth that she was not immune to the vicious disease of racism. How can the two extremes be present in the same person? Do they cancel one another out? Was one side fake and the other side the real person? Or is it possible for a person to possess contradictions—the best and worst of what makes us human? And if you are a person who has inherited or otherwise possess such noxious beliefs, is it possible to wholesale change?

In my Confessions on Humanity, I explore the complex yet simple nature of what it is to be human as an individual, on a collective basis, and as a spiritual whole. Turns out, we all have a heck of a lot in common.

Confessions

Confession #1: Original Sin: The Wicked Truth

I love you. You suck.

That's pretty much how the doctrine of Original Sin functions within popular American Christianity. God supposedly loves us as his crown jewel of creation but we also are born lowly, wicked, and insignificant. This is often referred to as Worm Theology thanks to several biblical references comparing humans to worms and subsequent theologians who capitalized on this notion.

I don't know about you but believing that I was a piece of shit just for being a living, breathing human didn't help me out too much in life. Nor was I empowered by the opposite belief, heralded by people reacting to the concept of Original Sin, that we are born with rainbows and unicorns flying out of our butts. The latter view is akin to the current parenting trend of giving every child a blue ribbon just for participating. It is inflated flattery and simply not realistic.

When I was in seminary, I was exposed to an interpretation of Original Sin that sought to revolutionize the age-old doctrine. The idea was that we should think of Original Sin as Original Woundedness. As my mother used to say, *Hurt people hurt people.* (The irony is not lost on me that she is the one who stood by for 10 years and sometimes literally watched as my stepdad beat us.)

While this notion is more palatable than worm theology, there are still at least a couple of problems with it. Firstly, what caused the original wounding in the first place? It is that causation that the doctrine of Original Sin seeks to explain, after all. Secondly, trying to reinvent a sucky doctrine by making it sound less offensive is as inadequate, ineffective and inflated as blue ribbons for the entire fourth grade.

We all have the capacity to live in grave darkness or illuminating light. We all have the capacity to do horrible things or beautiful things. We all have the capacity to elevate or debase our minds. We are inherently capable of *both* extremes.

Most of us live in a fluctuating middle though. Happiness is not found in this murky middle as evidenced by the societal epidemics of obesity, opioid addictions, and depression. As Americans, it is increasingly difficult to recognize our capacity for bottomless descension or limitless ascension. Our relative lives of ease prevent this. For most people, it is only through personally experienced challenge that we *choose* to either rise or fall.

Confession #2: Ego: I am People, People are Me

I had a boyfriend in my early 20s who was a medical student and a surfer, an intellectual with a hippie undercurrent. This was a couple of years after River Phoenix overdosed on a cocktail of drugs and alcohol and lost his life. One time, we were listening to Natalie Merchant's *River* and my boyfriend expressed how tragic his death was.

My reply was curt, "Well, if you choose to do drugs then that is a natural risk you take."

I think my boyfriend immediately questioned if I had a black hole for a heart.

In my mind, I was just being rational but it was actually my Ego trying to prove my worth. What was really happening in that scenario was that I had attached a sense of importance and superiority to the fact that I thought I had overcome childhood abuse without succumbing to drugs. If I could do that, then surely River Phoenix could have elected not to get all mired in drugs too and consequently he would not have died.[iii]

My response revealed a few things about me. I was woefully ignorant about issues that might lead to a drug overdose. I lacked compassion. I had not lived River Phoenix's life so who was I to judge? And most humbling, I had not triumphed over childhood trauma like I self-righteously thought I had. My residual problems were just different than drug abuse and would force a reckoning on me later in life.

I had a frail ego that worked overtime trying to make me feel better about myself.

It is a tricky subject slinging terms like ego and mind around because they are defined differently by authorities in different disciplines. Copious amounts of research and studies exist to substantiate the various interpretations of these words. So I will define how I intend these words in the context of spiritual discussion.

The mind is like your internal processor that sorts information, perceptions, and experiences and is the tangible source of consciousness. It is biologically linked to the brain; although some scientists now posit that the essence and functionality of the mind transcend the pure physicality of that organ.[iv]

The Ego, with a capital E, runs amuck in your mind and takes on a life of its own. It is fueled by Fear and serves itself and itself only, seeking constant validation. The Ego is the source of negative self-talk that destroys you. It is also the source of arrogant self-talk that artificially inflates you.

The mind can elevate or destroy you depending on how it identifies itself. If the Ego feeds the mind, it will destroy you. If Love feeds the mind, it will transform you.

Various religions and traditions approach this concept in their own unique ways. For example, Buddhism uses a catchy little description of "Monkey Mind" to describe the self-cannibalization power of the mind. Imagine the inner workings of your mind being overrun by an onslaught of nervously busy monkeys wreaking havoc with your thoughts. The Christian tradition speaks to the idea of renewing or transforming your mind away from the things of this world and toward Christ. I used to attend Al-Anon and it is there that I first heard the phrase *stinkin' thinkin'* and they weren't referring to deodorant! Behind all three of these examples is the root idea that our Egos can corrupt our minds, which affects everything else about our lives.

The immediate relevance of the Ego (and by extension, the mind) in our present discussion is this: We all have one.

Awareness of the Ego levels the playing field. This awareness, our God-space, is where we know that no one person is of greater or lesser value than another. My Ego told me I was less than other people when I saw Brooke Shields on the cover of a magazine when I was a young teen. It told me I was of lesser value than the girls in middle school who turned their backs on me at the lunch table. It told me I was superior to River Phoenix and superior to the ladies who attended that church small group I led.

33

If you start to listen, you will hear your Ego messing with your mind too. This is not a peaceful place. But in accepting the reality of our Ego, we are liberated to tame it. I celebrate the awareness of my Ego because it makes me one with my human family. We are all vulnerable to its cunning entrapments. Knowing this allows me to be more gracious to myself and others.

Confession #3: Dynamic Duo: Body & Spirit

Are we spiritual beings trapped in physical bodies?
Or, are we merely biological creatures made of dust that returns to dust?

Is your body a temple, as it is popular for some Christians to say?
Or, is it to be denigrated like other Christians say?

How much of your physical appearance constitutes *you*?

These questions have plagued me for most of my adult life. In my 20s, I went to work in lycra and spandex but spent my evenings reading and contemplating these and other existential questions. The dichotomy of working in the fitness industry while my deepest interests were in philosophy and spirituality exaggerated these dualities for me.

Going to seminary just muddied the waters when I was exposed to an abundance of theological theories on this matter. Pre-existentialism posits that we have souls that exist before our physical bodies. Traducianism claims we inherit our souls from our parents. Trichotomy says we are comprised of three parts: body, soul and spirit—and Dichotomy says that we are made of two parts—body and spirit. Of course, there is a slew of other theories, as well.

That is all these are. Theories. Not only that, these are theories about things that usually cannot be proven nor disproven. These theories seek to explain things that don't otherwise have an obvious explanation.

Rather than getting tangled in age-old conundrums, I came to a simple, satisfactory understanding. (At least for me.) It goes like this—

34

We have physical bodies. We are to care for those physical bodies to the best of our abilities out of appreciation and gratitude for the gift of life.

Yet there is a dimension of us as humans that transcends our physical bodies. This is the space whereby we are able to overcome Fear with Love, sorrow with joy and chaos with peace. This is the space where we see the Whole instead of just the self. Consciously living in this space grants humans the sense of place and purpose we deeply desire and fuels us with Love. Some people call this the God-space, some people think of it in different terms. It really doesn't matter.

Before you start farting rainbows, we return again ultimately to the mercy of our biological bodies. (Adult acne is proof that our bodies can sometimes have a mean sense of humor!) And you know the only other thing that is as certain as paying taxes.

Guess what? The story isn't over. Even after your death, the energy that you invested in this world multiplies for better or worse in the lives and situations that you left behind.

We are biology. We are MORE than biology. And we are to be good stewards of all that constitutes our being.

Confession #4: People Are Complex. People Are Simple.

To paraphrase Alfred North Whitehead, the only simplicity to be trusted is found on the far side of complexity. I have danced this internal tension most of my life, slipping in and out of the thick weight of burdensome complexity and then gliding into crystallized simplicity only to be pulled back down again and on the dance goes.

Christianity never worked to free me from this vicious cycle. There are two primary reasons Christianity fails in this arena. As a religion, it has historically sought to redeem the whole person. The problem is that neither religion nor the church is equipped to deal with biological or psychological issues humans may have. Coercing a person to say they believe X, Y, or Z doctrine will not cure addictions or reform an abuser, for example. Christianity needs to stay in its lane of spiritual development and not make claims about things of which it has no command.

Secondly, popular Christianity often reduces the complexity of our human experience to the notion that we are a) wretched, deplorable sinners, and b) just need to "give our lives to Jesus" and all will be well. I address the ineptitude of these pat platitudes in the next chapter on beliefs.

So after a lifetime of contemplation, I have come to terms with how I understand both the complexity and simplicity of being human. Let's see if I can explain both in plain terms beginning with simplicity.[v]

Simplicity

Aside from basic physical provisions (food, water, shelter, clothing, etc.), there are two simple needs of humanity: To have a sense of place and purpose and to love and be loved.

Complexity

The complexities of being human are structured like a four-strata pyramid. At the very base is *biology*. If a person has a physical or mental disability, chronic illness, intersex genes and organs, hereditary addiction or any host of biological issues, a fundamental challenge lies within their being. Such challenges may affect other tiers of the pyramid.

On top of this concrete stratum are the *experiences* we have from living. These may be either pronounced or recessed experiences. Pronounced experiences happen directly to or with you. Recessed experiences exist around you, creating more of an impression than a direct impact.

The combination of biology and experiences culminate in the next layer—that of the *lenses* through which we view ourselves, others, and the world around us. These lenses are mental constructs that exist to create efficient means to navigate life.

```
              /\
             /  \
            / Ego \
           /_____\
          /        \
         /  Lenses   \
        / Culmination of \
       / Biology & Experience \
      /_____\
     /                      \
    /      Experiences        \
   /    Pronounced or Recessed  \
  /_____\
 /                                \
/            Biology                \
/  Physiological Needs, Impairments, Conditions \
/_____\
```

Complexity of Being Human

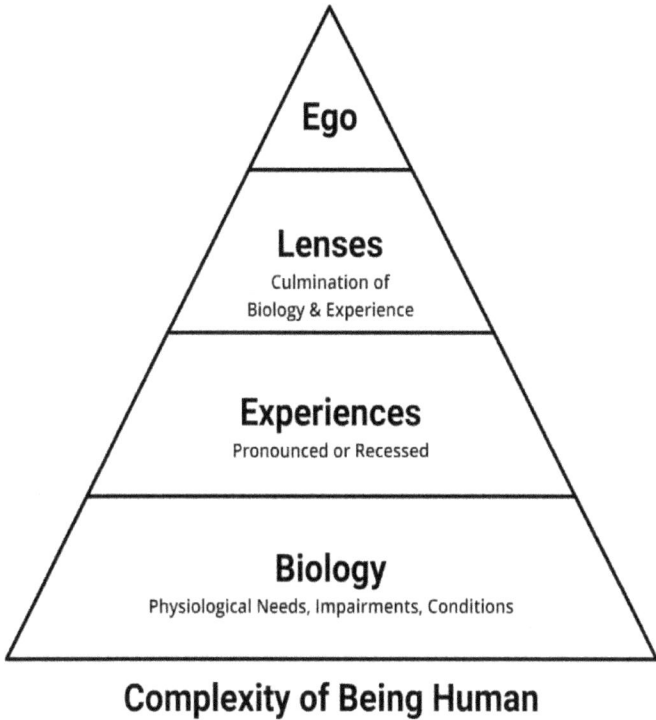

At the top of the pyramid rests the primary mechanism that creates a burdensome life of complexity for us as individuals and as a society. Say hello to my little friend... my Ego. The Ego is constantly scanning the lower strata looking for ways to muck us up. It creates internal dialogues and manufactures narratives to keep us fear-based and self-centered. It creates lenses that divide and destroy, interprets experiences as that which makes us victims, and usually has an extreme relationship with our biology, either loathsome or indulgent.

The good news is when Love replaces the Ego, then the complexities of what makes us human cease to be used against ourselves or others. The complexities no longer define us. Love defines us. In turn, our complexities can become an impetus or platform by which we may connect with others and elevate our communities. Love also allows us to understand our complexities as merely different shades of the same human condition as others, thereby fostering humility and graciousness. When the conversion from Ego to Love takes place, our place and purpose is centered on Love bringing us back to the simplicity of being human.

The reality, however, is that many people live in a vacillating space between Ego and Love. If we return to the story about my grandmother being a latent racist, this is a prime illustration. She did not have any significant biological challenges but she was entirely susceptible to the recessed experience of growing up in the early 20th century, Deep South racist culture. She inherited a collective ego-centric belief (her lens) about the supposed value differences between white and black people. All she knew was that worldview and it was substantiated by institutionalized discrimination, including by the church.

She had never been challenged enough to overcome those beliefs that were deeply instilled in her. Yet while my grandmother was a product of her time and place in history as it regards race relations, she was also a deeply loving and caring human who made the world a much better place for countless people. She desired nothing short of being the hands and feet of Jesus on this earth, even if she was unable to see the log in her own eye.[vi]

Confession #5: Interconnection: We Are People

Did you know that the world's heaviest and oldest living organism resides in Utah? Weighing in at over 6,600 tons and accumulating over 80,000 years of golden glory, the Pando Aspen Grove in Fishlake National Forest holds this distinction.[vii] What appears to be a forest of 40,000 individual trees is actually a singular organism united by a shared root system deep in the earth. The trees are just visible individual expressions of the same organism. The average lifespan of a tree is between 50 to 150 years. The root system generates the life force for propagation of a new generation of trees.

Researchers and arborists are concerned about the Pando cluster's future though. This is due to disease and insects and the lack of regeneration because of the overpopulation of plant-eating animals who eat the young aspens. The common root system allows for both the magnificence of the grove's natural beauty but also the disease that affects its entirety.

Long before I had learned of the unique singular root of the aspen species, an awareness dawned within me that humans are one organism, not 7.6 billion individual organisms. We are made One by our common nature. Our need for place and purpose, to love and be loved, and our inherent capacity for both goodness and malevolence is non-discriminatory. Indeed there are individual expressions (persons), like the aspen trees, that may demonstrate greater health or sickness than others but at the root of it all, we are the same. And when the root is infected we are all affected.

The primary thing that separates us are self-created constructs giving us the illusion that we are not One. Follow me along on a thought experiment.

Josh and Buddy grow up on opposite sides of a small Southern town. They play football against each other as high school rivals, each mocking the other and viewing him with disdain. It turns out that both Josh and Buddy win football scholarships to the same university. Initially, they hated each other during pre-season but their coach would have none of that and made them work it out. They came to realize their commonality as teammates and respect their mutual pursuit to be the best. They looked back at their high school prejudices with embarrassment.

Josh and Buddy join the military after college and both get deployed to the Middle East to fight in a decades-long war. They perceive another soldier, Lou, in their unit to be particularly obnoxious. He is from the inner city back home in the northeast. His brash mannerisms, unfamiliar slang, and unapologetic opinions fortify Josh and Buddy's friendship. They were comfortable with one another but not Lou, who represented an entirely different culture.

Until the day that Buddy's foot got blown off by a landmine and it was Lou who risked his life to pull Buddy out of the crossfire and bring him to safety. Buddy expressed his fear of dying and Lou, with the clarity of a divine messenger, exhorted him to stay present and claim his own life. After the current battle had ceased, Josh joined the pair and they waited for a helicopter evacuation. The three of them decry the horror of war and reminisce about home back in the United States.

A bond was formed between the three as a result of shared trauma. Instantly the differences weren't so important because they were united simply by their shared humanity. And a shared opponent. They fought side by side against their Middle Eastern adversaries.

Until... invaders from outer space (go with me here, it's a thought experiment!) blow up all government infrastructures around the planet. These pesky extraterrestrials effectively wipe out any semblance of borders or nations. They are looking to steal the earth's water supply for their own use.

Quickly it devolves into humans versus aliens. Josh, Buddy, and Lou are forced to work with their former war enemies in order for the human species to survive. In doing so, they discover the shared heartache, pain and joy of the human experience in the people who used to be vilified as "the other."

And this is where my thought experiment comes to a speedy close because I am immediately tempted to somehow place Brad Pitt and Will Smith somewhere in the storyline. I'm sure you get my point though. We draw arbitrary circles around ourselves (often that are fortified by the misuse of religion). These circles disintegrate when our experiences illuminate our shared humanity.

The interconnectedness of our human nature manifests in our actions and by our ancestry. Matt Damon does a phenomenal job of illustrating the interconnection of our actions in his monologue in *Good Will Hunting* in which he explains why he won't accept a job at the National Security Agency. He concludes by saying that he might as well just "shoot my buddy, take his job [and] give it to his sworn enemy, hike up gas prices, bomb a village, club a baby seal, hit the hash pipe, and join the National Guard." How can the first action (taking the job) end in clubbing a baby seal? (This is not an indictment of the N.S.A. by yours truly—just an illustration.)

All the issues that we think are not *our* issues are indeed our issues once we understand that we are One Human Family—homelessness, poverty, abuse, mental illness, addiction, the list could go on. While these things may not have a direct effect on your personal life, they all weave together as part of the fabric of the society in which we live.

We are also interconnected through our ancestry, both our direct lineage and collectively. For example, I was exposed to my grandmother's inherited racism and to the culture of my youth that was itself a contradictory amalgam of inherited racist beliefs and contemporaneous challenges to those beliefs. Both influences shaped me. Another example is addiction. If you or someone you love has addiction in their family tree, it becomes vividly apparent how generational illness can continue into perpetuity unless one is resolved to be a part of the solution.

If we examine our own lives, it is hopeful that we can discover instances where we allowed boundaries to be dissolved and communion to take place with those who otherwise seemed different from us.

Confession #6: First World Problems/First World Responsibility

Many people who have heard my life story think that I have endured great adversity. I would not disagree with that, particularly relative to our society. But I have never known what it is like not to have clean drinking water. I do not know what it is like to live in a culture that denies me based on the pigment of my skin. I have never had to flee my country out of fear of ethnic cleansing. My children have not been ripped from my embrace and hatcheted to death before my eyes. These are very real things that people all around the world endure.

By contrast, my present life is radically different. I have an iPhone, live in a comfortable home, drive a nice car, get mani/pedis once a month, eat healthy, delicious food and binge-watch Netflix. I feel safe in my man's arms and our children find refuge in our home. I have a snarky cat and a flatulent, adoring dog.

In the course of my personal and graduate studies, I became acutely aware of the disparity within the world. In the past, I have wasted immeasurable time and energy feeling immobilized with guilt for the relative security I have in the United States. I was never in a position to directly change those global atrocities and my life often felt vain in comparison.

I think many people in our country live with this awareness. Often we are tempted to treat it like the elephant in the corner because we feel powerless to affect any real change. Besides, if we fully embrace the reality of other people's sufferings, we have to face our own priorities that oftentimes are indulgent. So we continue on our merry way of buying more clothes, eating bigger portions, and losing ourselves to digital vapidity.

We often joke about #firstworldproblems when the Wi-Fi doesn't work or it takes too long for the barista to make our skinny, no foam, caramel macchiato, or when we have to fly coach on an economy airline. Those are embarrassing examples of first-world problems with a small p. I call the discrepancy between our life of ease and luxury with the hardship and poverty of the rest of the world *The* First-World Problem with a capital P.

The First-World Problem is on glorious display at many American Christian churches.

I have been to churches where the services are produced like a Broadway musical. Every few weeks when the pastor changes his sermon series (it's always a guy) then the elaborate set is exchanged for another elaborate set. There is usually a highly produced video that is played on a jumbotron that extols the latest mission trip or someone's conversion to the faith. A rock band fit to blow the roof off a football stadium bangs out worship songs swelling the audience to an emotional high, only to bring them down with a dramatic decrescendo filling the theater with a potent hush—as if God had been holding his breath and finally exhaled. There is no telling the human and material resources needed to pull all of this off.

I am intentionally using theater terminology here. This entertainment-centric approach amongst American churches has a direct correlation to our country's affluence and consumerist culture. It also reflects a church worried about maintaining the attention of its audience. (Read: Fear-based.)

The problem is what people *really* want is not more entertainment. Church as entertainment is akin to people who distract themselves by buying more stuff, eating more, etc. What we really want is a sense of place and purpose and to love and be loved. Besides, if these diversionary tactics were working, there wouldn't be 4,000 people a day defecting from Christianity and you probably wouldn't be reading this book.

Whether we are talking about The First-World Problem on an individual or collective level (like the Church), we share A First-World Responsibility. That responsibility entails recognizing that we are One Human Family and we must do our individual and collective parts to elevate others who suffer.

Confession #7: The Choice

Fear is the problem.

Love is the Solution.

People are the conduit for either.

The choice between the two is the ultimate question we must all ask ourselves. This is the beginning of a changed life and a changed world.

The Dovetail: Parting Thoughts, Summations and a Send-Off

A Change is Gonna Come

One day in October of 1963, Sam Cooke arrived in my hometown of Shreveport, Louisiana where he was scheduled to perform the following evening. The hotel where he had reservations refused to accommodate him, his wife, and his entourage. It was an obvious racist rejection.

Sam was understandably upset. His wife and brother had to calm him down because they feared that Sam would be killed. The group left to go to another hotel. Upon their arrival, the police were waiting and arrested them for disturbing the peace. Two months later, Cooke penned one of the most provocative and powerful social justice songs ever written.

If I were to pick one song that best captures the sentiment of my childhood, it would be Sam Cooke's *A Change is Gonna Come*. Cooke's pain and despair of systemic oppression and aggregated subhuman treatment fueled his passion in this song. While I can never know what it is to be African-American in the U.S., this song nonetheless stirs me deeply for multiple reasons.

For one thing, my mother often played soul music on her vinyl record player before she married my stepdad. We would lay on the gold shag carpet and listen to the sounds of Sam Cooke, Otis Redding, and Johnny Mathis, to name a few, while their soothing and sometimes haunting vocals filled the room. So I suppose I have a nostalgic connection with *A Change is Gonna Come*.

Secondly, despite the racist influences and general ignorance of my childhood, I somehow was aware that something just wasn't *right* about the social and economic divisions between the white and black communities in my town. Something felt wrong when we would drive through the cotton fields and I saw black children hanging out on the porch of a shanty on my way to my grandparents' house. It was like viewing an alternative universe from the outside, being struck by the incongruence of it, but not knowing what to do about it. *A Change is Gonna Come* is the soundtrack in my mind when I reflect on these memories. But it goes deeper than that.

When my mother got involved in a Christian cult and agreed to an arranged marriage to my stepfather, the divorce of my parents became the least of my problems. The stepfather element ushered in a 10-year season of extreme abuse, oppression, and psychological torment. While I do not know what it is like to experience systemic injustice due to the color of my skin, I do know what it is like to suffer, to be afraid to breathe the wrong way, to never be able to rest in your own home, to live in a constant double-bind where you incur abuse no matter what you do, to fear that those who should protect you will kill you, and to long with a wordless, vacuous groan, deep in your being, for a change to come.

The acuity of my suffering as a child heightened my sensitivity to the suffering of others. It motivated me to be the change I wanted to see in the world, as cliché as that sounds.

As One Human Family, we must understand that we are in this together. Unfortunately, people tend to learn best when they have direct experience with adversity before their eyes are opened to larger truths. I do not wish suffering on anyone. But I do exhort us all to take active measures to expand our personal arena. Seek out opportunities to grow, learn, and know people who are different than you. Both you and the world will be better off for it.

On Worms, Equity and First Wounds

Worms are people too!

Worms are often overlooked, left to dry out on the sidewalk after a hard rain. They seem insignificant in the grand scheme of things when our minds are obsessed with more pressing matters. But these same worms aerate the soil that allows water and oxygen to enrich it. The soil, in turn, grows the trees that give you shade, produces the crops that grew the lettuce on your turkey burger, and yields the flowers that you ordered on the internet to send to the chick that you are trying to impress with your awesomeness. They are food for the birds who poop the seeds of the wildflowers that vibrantly grow along the highway when you take that girl on a road trip to a rural B&B for a romantic adventure—one she will surely never forget thanks to you, your awesomeness and well, worms.

Come to think of it, maybe I don't mind being compared to a worm. I am just one of billions of others just like me trying to do my part to make the world a better place. (Take that, Calvin!)[viii] This Right View of self—as neither greater than nor less than other people—frees us to create an equitable world.[ix] We all share in the best and worst of what makes us human.

All of the -isms and -phobias that plague our culture are equal-opportunity culprits. Racism, ageism, sexism, homophobia (it goes on and on) do not discriminate as to whom they may burrow their insidious grip. We must admit that our shared human nature, when in a ripe circumstance, makes us all *capable* of such of-fenses. This is readily apparent in the highly polarized political climate of our time. Intolerance, hate, deceit, and shitty behavior isn't exclusive to one party or another. The solution requires us to see the Love in one another and take action on principles greater than our individual self-interests.

There is one caveat though. I call it First Wound Responsibility. There are often circumstances, on every scale, that do not have easy, clear-cut answers. For example, the complexity of how to heal a fractured society still marred by racism has cultural, practical, normative, and systemic tentacles that have no easy fix. I am not a social scientist, politician, or policy maker but I do know this: when all else has been considered and the path is still not clear, those in power should assume First Wound Responsibility when determining the solution, whether or not they individually contributed to the problem. This means that when there are two or more options of recourse and they all seem legitimate in their own right, the balance should be tipped in favor of the person or group of persons who suffered the First Wound. The decimation of the native people of this continent and the enslavement of Africans brought to the United States by white European settlers are tragic epitomes of societal First Wounds.

I've Come a Long Way, Baby!

I still haven't hooked a worm to this very day. However, by the time I was in college I was the only Caucasian young woman to be asked to speak at the annual Martin Luther King, Jr. celebration due to my active involvement on campus initiating opportunities that brought people of all origins together for common activities and purpose. Following that speech, I was honored to be invited to join Delta Sigma Theta, a historically and predominantly African-American women's sorority. Much to my forty-something-year-old regret, I had declined. At the time, I thought of myself as too independent to join any sorority but if I had, it definitely would have been Delta Sigma Theta. I can only imagine how that experience would have expanded me as a human. It may be a pale consolation, but since that time I have been involved in countless initiatives that seek to break down barriers and build unity while transcending labels.

I am grateful that I can carry forward the abundance of goodness that my grandmother imparted to me. I am also grateful that I can shatter the lenses she had inherited that promoted division rather than unity of our One Human Family. We have the ability to transform our lives beyond the artificial constructs we inherit when we allow Love as God to be our power and our orientation.

Our beliefs shape our thinking and actions. Often they do not positively serve us or others until they are challenged to change.

Are you up for a challenge? To the chapter on beliefs, we now go!

CHAPTER 3

BELIEFS

We didn't celebrate Halloween growing up. That was the "devil's holiday." So this was our Fall Festival. I'm the eggplant.

Opener: What Goes Around Comes Around

Have you ever had sex in your parents' bed? I have. And it's probably not what you think.

When I was in elementary school, my greatest sliver of happiness was going to ballet lessons twice a week. Ballet was an intrinsic pull for me the way that some people are born musicians or inventors. I was good at it and dreamed of being a professional dancer.

But in my third year of lessons, my stepdad grew increasingly wary of the enterprise. He found multiple ways and opportunities to communicate two stringent beliefs he had about my love for dance. He said that if I remained in the world of theater, I would most assuredly become either demonic or gay. The dramatic arts are "Satan's playground."

To my fifth grade ears, it was like someone gesturing wildly and yelling in my face, eyeballs bulging and spit flying sideways, "Run for dem hills! Evil's a'comin'! Run, dagnabit, run!" Only to find a duck waddling around the corner. All I wanted to do was pirouette to Tchaikovsky. But his propaganda shamed me into "voluntarily" quitting.

He may have made me quit ballet but years later I had lesbian sex in his bed. And guess what? The world, indeed, did not come to an end. The real destructive bedfellows are hate and ignorance.

Menu and Music: Eat Your Veggies

I'm assigning veggies to this chapter because vegetables are nutrient-rich and essential for a healthy, balanced diet. Similarly, the beliefs that we hold can enrich our lives or destroy them or the lives of others if they are toxic. If french fries and ketchup are your mainstays for getting your veggies, then your (ill) health will reflect that. We must put nutrient-rich foods in our bodies and possess rational, healthy beliefs in our minds.

There is no better song for the Chapter on Beliefs than one of the most celebrated gay anthems for drag shows across the country, *Believe* by Cher. Play it loud, play it proud! Channel your inner drag queen or better yet, invite a real one over for dinner. After all, who can turn down *Believe in Love Veggies?*

The Backstory: The Pearl in the Oyster

Ok, so I'm not advocating for revenge sex but allow me to tell you why it is that I ended up playing Hello Kitty in my stepfather's bed and what that has to do with religious beliefs.

The cult network that my mom and stepdad were a part of taught that all people were to be servants to their shepherd.[x] The shepherd was the conduit to God on your behalf. This man— because it was only men who were shepherds—dictated how you dressed, where you could or could not go, who you could or could not speak to, and what you could or could not do.

It was like a multi-level marketing scheme where everyone bottle-necked at the top with one man who had direct access to God. The farther you were down the pyramid, the more SOL you were. Women and children comprised the base of the pyramid. Being a female child, I was doubly SOL.

My stepfather was my "shepherd" until presumably one day I would get married and the shepherd mantle would pass to my husband. Not only did my stepfather physically, verbally and psychologically abuse me, I was also sexualized by him. He would make me pose for him in swimsuits, walk for him in jeans so he could assess my ass, and strip me down to my panties before beating me.

But that wasn't the worst of what happened.

I was sexually abused by an elder in the church when I was about six years old. This man had a daughter my age, and I frequently spent the night at their house when we were in early elementary school. He worked for a local shoe store by day but was a revered leader in the church dispensing spiritual bile and micromanaging other people's lives in his off-time. He would come into his daughters' bedroom where I would be sleeping to "check the air conditioner." (His house had window units.) What he really checked were the contours of my vagina after he pulled my panties down.

But that wasn't the worst of what happened.

I was plagued with nightmares for years. I slept with my legs tightly crossed and felt a simmering anger inside of me but didn't understand why. When I began to go through puberty, I was repulsed by my own body and the changes that were happening "down there."

At 16, I finally told my mom what happened to me 10 years earlier. Being a dutiful cult-wife, she said to me, "You need to tell your father," meaning my stepfather. This made me sick because I feared him and somehow didn't expect things to go well. But what I had to say was the truth so surely I was doing the right thing by coming forward.

My stepdad cross-examined me like I was a murder suspect. He reiterated to me what a man of God "Milton" was and how serious my allegations were. He said that he would talk to the head pastor of the church and get back to me.

Days passed. I waited, stomach in knots, every footstep on pins and needles. I was anticipating a great pronouncement and some sort of relief. Finally, I prompt my mom who prompts my stepdad to circle back around with me on this little matter.

He sat me down and said, "You know, Milton has been going through a tough time lately. He got laid off. We just don't think this is a good time to deal with this." I knew what this meant—it was a dead issue.

My heart sank like a lead vault to the bottom of the ocean, taking all of its hidden contents with it.

But that still isn't the worst of what happened.

A couple of months later, my mom and stepdad invited Milton and his wife over for coffee and Christian fellowship, as it was called. I was charged with serving Milton, refilling his cup and offering him his choice of Sweet'N Low or sugar—all with the requisite smile on my face.

THAT is the worst of what happened.

This story can be unpacked on many levels, peeling back the layers of implicit beliefs about children, females, male dominance, sexuality, and religion. But none of that is the point I want to make right now.

What you believe affects the way that you live. And how you live can really fuck with someone else's life.

In my case, the sexual abuse act was not the most egregious example of sexual abuse by a long shot. But the denial of my person as a whole being and the shame of being penalized for being a victim carried forward into my life for many years. I lost my virginity at age 17 to a 25 year-old and had a string of sexual encounters afterwards in the empty pursuit of finding a man who wouldn't harm me and who would love me. The wolves prey on the wounded.

By the time I was in college, I could not cite one positive male relationship that I had in my life other than the distant affection that I had for my grandfather. I was a lamb drowning at sea being swallowed by the appetite of a rabid world. I had no functional parents and by all accounts was surviving on my own. More than anything I was lonely. I craved love like vegetation craves sunlight.

And then it hit me. Think outside the cock, Rachel! Maybe I've been looking for love in all the wrong places. I knew two things. I didn't want to be lonely and I was open-minded. I (still) didn't know what a clitoris was, much less what lesbianism was about, but I was willing to find out.

I'll tell you more about what my LUG years (Lesbian Until Graduation) taught me about sexuality, compassion and the human family in my Confession on Sexuality below. For now, I need to tie up the loose end about doing it with another chick in my stepdad's bed.

Shortly before the divorce of my mom and stepdad when I was a senior in college, I brought my girlfriend to my hometown for a weekend visit. To everyone else though, she was my "roommate." She was an elegant, young, African-American woman. I was definitely pushing the threshold of tolerance in this white-bread, bologna town.

My parents were out of town and let us stay in their house—the house of my childhood. We could have slept in any room that weekend but both agreed that there was some sort of poetic justice by sleeping in the master bedroom.

This was the same bed, with the same wretched bedspread, where my stepdad used to lay me out and beat me up and down the back of my body. He would turn deep red, his black eyes narrowed with barbarous intensity, while sweat poured down his face as if emerging from a baptism of cruelty. His instruments of choice ranged from thick boards and paddles, to belts, boots, cables, or switches. Sometimes he invoked God during his beatings, sometimes not.

My motivation was not revenge as you might think. I wanted to prove a cosmic truth. My stepdad was the kind of man who would aggressively leave a restaurant, in a self-righteous furor, if he suspected our server was gay. He wanted to see gay people dead. It was as if he thought gay people were infected with some sort of biological weapon that would annihilate the earth. He also was a racist who thought that there were *some* black people who were good people. So I knew that if I slept in his bed with my black girlfriend and had lesbian sex (for good measure) that nothing, absolutely *nothing,* would come of it and he would never know the difference.

Confessions

Confession #1: The Bible: A Beautiful Mess

When I was in seminary, I attended a brown bag lecture series in which two professors took an hour to delineate why the Bible doesn't, in fact, condemn homosexuality. They traced etymologies of ancient Hebrew and Greek words, extrapolated on biblical texts and maneuvered their way to the sweeping conclusion that the Bible loves and supports gay people. Roll out the rainbow flags and cue the Cher!

I left more annoyed than informed. If it takes an hour of intellectual shenanigans to justify your position then something is wrong, particularly when the Bible is quite clear in its adversarial orientation to homosexuality.[xi] And if it takes having a PhD to manufacture such an argument then the wrongness is compounded. I remember a particular professor who had written multiple papers and books defending the acceptance of homosexuality within the Bible. With preposterous flair, she once declared that she was done entertaining anyone who didn't already understand how the Bible clearly wasn't anti-gay, as if her resigning from this fight proved something.

I have a simpler solution.

Why not just admit that the Bible is *wrong* on the matter of homosexuality?

The Bible is a human-made object, a collection of books, laws, poetry, letters and other manuscripts. Scholars estimate that these texts were written from roughly 1500 BCE to 100 CE. It chronicles the spiritual, cultural and moral evolution of the Jewish people and early Christians, the latter of whom adopted and theologically retrofitted the Hebrew scriptures. The final collection of Catholic Christian books was not canonized until the late 4th century CE. The Orthodox Christian tradition developed a slightly different canon. In 1517, Martin Luther's unintended spawning of the Protestant revolution furthered edits to the Catholic canon, subsequently creating the Protestant Christian Bible.

To illustrate the fluidity and human-nature of the Bible, other Christian groups have felt the need to supplement or improve upon the Protestant Bible. For example, the Church of Jesus Christ of Latter-day Saints views the Bible as being quite flawed due to translation and scribal errors over the years. They view their Book of Mormon, first published in 1830, to be the unaltered Word of God. Jehovah's Witnesses believe that *their* translation of the Bible is the only correct translation. And if you would have talked to my grandmother, she would have told you that the King James Version was *the* accurate version.

There is no "original Bible" out there somewhere. Rather, there are fragments of ancient texts from scattered sources that contemporary biblical scholars rely upon to trace the authenticity of translations. Most modern Bibles are based upon translations of translations of translations that originate at a dead end. There are no first sources available and scholars have verified hundreds of thousands of scribal and translational errors that have long been codified in modern Bibles.

Trust me, my three-paragraph synopsis of the evolution of the Bible is a gross simplification. A quick Google search will inundate you with the enormity of the subject. My concern here is to spare you the deep research and the need for a doctorate in Biblical Studies. I'd rather get straight to the point and launch a cultural revolution on this matter instead.

What is needed is a Right View of the Bible. It is a collection of documents that reflects how ancient people came to understand their sense of place and purpose in the world and that which is greater than them, aka God. It can inform us about how ancient people sought answers to natural phenomena, geography, civic and moral life, anthropology, history, and spirituality. It is full of contradictions, outmoded thinking, and misnomers but it is also full of wisdom, insight and ultimate truth.

Like the humanity that it reflects, the Bible should not be discounted as wholly flawed nor should it be revered as wholly flawless. Just because there are inaccuracies and antiquated values doesn't mean that there is not truth present in other areas. The two extremes are not mutually exclusive.

Also, much like humanity, it is complicated and simple at the same time. It is complex with its layers of composition, translations, revisions, genres, and cultural contexts. It is simple in its embodiment of the human existential yearning for connection to Something Greater: LOVE.

The approach to the Bible is the doctrinal root problem with most of American Christianity today, particularly evangelicalism. People worship the Bible when they think they are worshipping God.

More specifically, they are worshipping their particular interpretation of the Bible and retrofitting their God to it. Or they construct their God and cherry-pick the Bible to support it. Either way, it's the same tactic. Both conservative evangelicals and progressive liberals (to a lesser degree) do this. We could all lay down our arms if we had a Right View of the Bible.

The fact that two diametrically opposed groups both cite the same book to justify their God and hence their agendas, tells us two chief things.[xii] The Bible is a tool. The intention of how to use the tool begins and ends with people.

Seeing the Bible for what it is, with its inherent flaws, its transcendent wisdom, and the tension between the two, does not demote the Bible. It becomes no less sacred a text. I would even argue that the Bible would become more sacred to more people if we could embrace the truth about it. I find no sacredness in intentional ignorance, misrepresentations, or denial of facts.

I prefer to appreciate the sacred within reality.

Confession #2: The Trinity: Fuzzy Math

Ok, let's be honest. If you were raised a Christian, chances are you learned very little about the doctrine of the Trinity. Why? Because it doesn't even make sense to those Christians who feel the need to defend it.

1+1+1=1 Got it? Father, Son and Holy Spirit: all one God. *Not* separate beings—rather, one being of the same substance but three expressions.

The Trinity is not an explicit doctrine in the New Testament. Rather, it is a doctrine that had to be hammered out over the course of a few hundred years in early Christendom with bishops, saints and popes getting their robes all knotted over words like begotten, co-eternal and consubstantial. People were banished, excommunicated and killed over their stance on this doctrine. The interpretation that finally won out, as formalized in the Nicene Creed, was a result of political savvy and might.

Here's the great irony: A common modern interpretation of The Trinity is that it speaks to the primacy of Relationship as illustrated in what is called the Godhead (Father, Son, Holy Spirit). This is to be a model for harmonious relationships for humans. Yet, much strife, castigation and destruction ensued amongst Christian leaders during this doctrine's formative years. Apparently similar tumult seeps into modern times, too.

I had such an experience in seminary. (This was an early signal that I was on the rapid road to becoming a None.) The classroom was small with about 12 students. The tables were arranged like a rectangle with the professor seated at the front of the room. We were reading ancient writings from early Christian fathers on the subject of the Trinity. The professor moderated student debates about the merits of different positions.

One particular day, the subject of the role of the Holy Spirit was at hand. Micro factions within the classroom began to surface with students holding firm to their favored position. Zeal escalated quickly with academically guised insults being traded for dogmatic indictments. Even the professor had to sit back in his chair, eyes like saucers, while the classroom took on an intensity of its own.

I felt like I was in the middle of a giant theological circle jerk. The only thing being proven in this exchange was that Egos are like lube—it lathers things up to the point where something is going to explode. And as far as I was concerned, they were all shooting blanks.

It might as well have been a fight about the jolly guy that lives at the North Pole.

"Santa is definitely human. A human with magical powers but definitely a human," states Student A.

"No, Santa is an elf," retorts Student B.

"Actually," says Student C, "Santa is more like an uber elf, twice the size of regular elves but with elf DNA."

"No, he is human as evidenced by his Type 2 diabetes due to all those cookies, you moron." Student A says with a take-that emphasis.

"He has the essence of an elf but nature of a human!" Student D says trying to broker some peace and feel relevant in the conversation.

Slow to follow the volleys, a starry-eyed Student E muses, "How do you know he has Type 2?"

But before Student A could delineate his knowledge of Santa's medical condition, Student B interjects with a booming voice drowning all opposition, "Listen all you apostates! *'Twas the Night Before Christmas* clearly states he is a 'right, jolly old elf.' The poem says it, I believe it, that's that!"

A loud silence crashes to the floor.

A wayward cricket, trapped indoors, chirps helplessly to be let out.

Then Student F, who never speaks up, mutters, "Well technically the word *elf* is a mistranslation from the original text. So I don't know..." he trails off.

Hang me with a candy cane and pummel me with sugar plums, puh-*leeze*.

What struck me most about this conversation was not that there were differing views on the *meaning* of the Trinity but rather, that students were staking supernatural claims about occurrences that supposedly actually happened—claims that are no more credible than the existence of Santa Claus.

There are indeed many interpretations of The Trinity that are meaningful. Generally, they center around the importance of relationships, interdependence, and mutuality and/or seek to explain the different facets of the Christian God.

However, hm mmm, a doctrine that causes confusion and division rather than clarity and unity simply needs to be dropped or at the very least put into perspective that it is an ancient way to explain something otherwise unexplainable.

Love is God. Love brings together—not tears apart—particularly in the name of God! How about we just speak directly about the redeeming meaning *behind* the doctrine? People who place doctrine above Love worship doctrine, not God.

Drop the doctrine. Keep the meaning.

Confession #3: Jesus

I make a mean chicken pot pie. The bottom and top crusts are flaky and oh-so-tender and the filling has roasted chicken, fresh herbs, and fresh veggies including onions, celery, carrots, green beans, peas and mushrooms. The gravy is creamy and seasoned to perfection. All in all, home cooked goodness that'll make you want to slap your mama!

If you're saying to yourself, I don't like chicken pot pie, then you've probably had one of those nasty ones that comes frozen in a little metal tray. The thin top crust is rock hard and flavorless. There is no bottom crust, which is an abomination. The chicken is a dark rubbery substance. (Is it *really* chicken??) The vegetables have a watery indistinct taste and the gravy is so loaded with sodium that you bloat 10 pounds just looking at it.

The original Jesus is like my pot pie: the real deal, genuinely nourishing and harder to come by. The manufactured Jesus that has been created by usually innocent, sometimes malevolent, and almost always unwitting humans over the past two millennia is like the frozen grocery store version, a far cry imitation with little nutritional value that has been mass-produced and leaves you unfulfilled.

If I could have a fantasy dinner date with Jesus, I would make him my chicken pot pie. I would also ask him, "What do you think about all the crazy stuff that humans have done in your name?"

Similar to the Bible, Jesus is a Rorschach test—what you see in it is a reflection of the beholder more than the image itself. If you have tribalist, exclusionary leanings, you will interpret a Jesus who supports that. If you have open-minded, inclusionary leanings, you will interpret a Jesus who supports that. It circles back again to one's understanding of the Bible and whether it should be taken literally or contextually. It probably goes without saying at this point, but I understand both the Bible and Jesus contextually.

Reframing my Jesusology, freed me to appreciate and revere Jesus for the significant cultural and spiritual figure that he was/is. I have lived and breathed every major facet of American Jesus that there is. I speak from experience and with conviction. Allow me to delineate what I came to reject about Jesus and what I have come to believe about Jesus.

Jesus was fully human, never intended to start a new religion, nor did he desire to be worshipped. And he thought you and I were divine as much as he was.

Phew. I just had to spit it out like that. Now I'll unpack it.

Jesus was human. He was not some external-otherness, cosmic deity that morphed into human form and roamed the earth. He was human like you and me. But he was an exceptional, enlightened human like Buddha, Lao Tzu, or any other number of spiritual luminaries that were lights on this earth.

He was turned into God by the humans who followed him (or more likely by the humans who followed the humans who followed the humans who followed Jesus and so on).

He was made God by humans for two primary reasons. Firstly, they didn't understand his primary message and secondly, it is human nature to deify someone because it deflects responsibility from ourselves.

Starting with the latter, Americans collectively do this all the time to politicians, celebrities, and sports figures. Individually, we often do the same to our romantic partners. We put these people up on pedestals to idolize but are quick to tear them apart if they fail our expectations. This arc is similar to our man JC who was abandoned by his own followers when he was apprehended by the authorities and executed.

Jesus' primary message can be summarized in one word: Love. We are to be Love, see Love in others, give Love, receive Love. Further, Jesus taught that this Love transcends societal, cultural, racial, religious and any other categories in which humans quarantine themselves. In participating in this Love, in the union with this Love, we all share divinity. In *this* way,

Jesus was God's son. Jesus fully recognized his own divinity. He recognized it in everyone else too.

It is that last little bit that humanity could not wrap its head around. To suggest that every person—regardless of any identifiers about them—is divine was the most radical statement possible in Roman-occupied Jerusalem in the first century CE. It remains the most radical statement today, too.

Jesus was not trying to initiate a new religion. He was not anti-Jewish. He was constrained by the vernacular and cultural constructs of his day. If anything, he was trying to reform Judaism. Yet his spiritual enlightenment transcended such temporal barriers. He was pro-Love during a time when the current religious establishment had become too politicized and self-seeking, which is exactly where American Christianity is today.

I think Jesus would be grieved to see the way humans turned his gospel of Love into the worship of him. I think he would be horrified to see the vast scale of abuse that has been propagated in his name, twisting a message of Love into an instrument of self-serving power.

Confession #4: Sexuality: Behind the Fig Leaf

When you think "sexuality" and "Christianity" in the same breath, what comes to mind?

The culmination of your mental, physical, and spiritual energies uniting in power, intensity, and mind-blowing pleasure with the one true love of your life that erupts as if all the stars in the universe suddenly exploded?

Nah, I didn't think so.

Let's try it again. When you think "sexuality" and "Christianity" in the same breath, what comes to mind?

Sexually repressed priests who take it out on little boys?

Televangelists who shout, "Come, Lord Jesus, Come!" while banging the organist's wife?

The lovely folks from Westboro Baptist Church who champion their "God Hates Fags" campaign?

Lois, the uptight, Bible-thumping, judgmental prude down the hall in the HR department that you wish would get laid ASAP so that she could chill for a minute?

Yeah, that's what I thought.

Much like I suggested in my Confession on the Bible, Christianity needs a hard reset when it comes to sexuality. The overarching problem is duplicity. The Christian beliefs about sexuality are not supported by the results. If we think that sexual abuse, infidelity, pornography, homosexuality and any other variation of what is rightfully or illegitimately labeled taboo doesn't involve American Christians at the same rate as the general public, then we are fooling ourselves. For one thing, Christians—or at least Christians by heritage—comprise the vast number of the general public. So any statistics about these cultural sexual manifestations by default include a vast swath of Christians.

My first thing to say to American Christianity is, "Get over yourselves."

Sexuality is a natural part of human existence that when treated with respect and love, is sublime. If more sanctimonious Christians understood this (and bumped nasties a few times a month), the world would be a much more relaxed place.

Secondly, let's allow science to do its job and Christianity should do what it claims to do—teach Love. Sexuality exists on a continuum and science bears this out. The rudimentary understanding of sexuality as purely a binary proposition is as blind as thinking your hands don't have germs just because you can't see them. Not only do many humans *experience* sexuality on a continuum (my LUG years are a great example) but this is *biologically* proven, too, and I would imagine, psychologically the case. A baby can be born with non-binary sex organs or conflicting sex chromosomes just like it's possible to be born with six toes or low white blood cell counts.

How many gay teens need to commit suicide because they are shamed by ineffective conversion therapy or rejected by their families? How many children need to be abused because of repressive traditions? How many marriages need to be eviscerated because there is not a healthy view of sexuality (or gender equality)? How many teens need to lose their virginity at Christian camps because the church demonstrates double standards about sex? How many adult men must continue living with implicit shame just because they feel a strong, carnal sexual impulse but have no acceptable outlet in the Christian bubble so they engage in otherwise destructive and secretive habits? How many women have to continue spending half their lives struggling between the expectation of being good enough to marry but naughty enough to be screwed?

Why can't we be whole beings that celebrate our sexuality as part of that whole?

Thirdly, the Church is revoltingly hypocritical. The Church has a weird fascination with people's sex lives. There is a prominent evangelical church in my city— let's call it "Watershark"— that has notoriously outed and ousted gay members who refuse to live celibately or abide by conversion therapy. While this church may have every right to make its own rules and enforce them, Watershark is a disgusting example of hypocrisy prevalent in evangelical churches. Watershark doesn't out and oust its heterosexual members who have sex outside of marriage. Most of American Christianity has a "don't ask, don't tell" policy to premarital heterosexual sex. Why? Probably because if the Church was consistent about ousting all of its deviant members, there would be no one left to pay tithes. (Mic drop.)

Hypocrisy also takes place amongst many "progressive churches" in more subtle forms. There are denominations who say that gay people are welcome in their churches but... just don't be open about being gay. We won't marry you or outwardly recognize your partner as your partner, but hey, you are welcome because we are sooooo open minded and cool.

I regularly served on the chancel in a liturgical service at a church, let's call it "Hilltop Methodist," while I completed my master's degree. There was an exceptionally talented organist who performed every Sunday. His husband attended church every Sunday as well. They had been married for over 15 years. (The wedding had taken place at a "gay church," not Hilltop.) Everyone knew they were husbands but no one ever acknowledged it.

The approach was kind of like the way some families may handle an awkward Thanksgiving scenario. Everyone saw the foot growing out of Uncle Larry's forehead but it was better just to pretend it wasn't there. Pass the gravy, please!

And if you were to try and get a straight answer (irony intended) from church leadership on its position on gay members, you would get some nebulous mumbo-jumbo that could be interpreted any way you wanted. (This doublespeak is quite common in mainline denominations who are waging internal battles about church policy and social issues.) At least places like Watershark make their positions readily known. I don't know what is worse, being executed in front of your congregation or suffering death by a thousand cuts via subtle insults and denials week by week.

Church, you have failed me and millions more Americans in helping shape whole people. Thank God I was a lesbian for a few years so that I could learn the things you didn't teach me—you know, things like compassion and love for all people.

The Rainbow Experience

My foray into the gay subculture occurred in the early '90s. This was on the cusp of a cultural revolution that eventually gained gay and lesbian people more legal rights, greater social acceptance, and heightened positive media presence. At that time in Texas though, the only places where gay people were free to be themselves were safe environments like certain universities and neighborhood enclaves that had organically become the "gay part of town."

The experience I had was like what I imagine a Witness Protection Program might be. Your identity changes, you are dropped into a culture that you know nothing about, you adopt the mores and customs, and you try to fit in. Only I didn't have to *try* to fit in because the gay and lesbian community that I knew was so welcoming, non-threatening and accepting. (Hint, hint: that's the way churches *should* be.)

Being a LUG (Lesbian Until Graduation) taught me more than what immediately comes to your dirty mind. Yes, I learned a ton about female sexuality that I would have been hard-pressed to learn otherwise. I learned about uniquely gay and lesbian cultural expressions. (There's some truth to the U-Haul joke!)[xiii] I came to appreciate drag performers and Whitney Houston on a whole other level. I learned that when driving, gay people go forward, not straight. I learned what a "beard" was. I learned that gay males have impeccable taste even on a low budget. (We were in college after all.)

While all of the above were interesting things to experience, as an outsider living inside, that was just the superficial layer. If you peel the onion, this experience eventually heightened my awareness of the human condition.

The Allure and Power of Tribe

When I was a college baby trying to figure myself out, I quickly acknowledged that choosing to "be gay" (because for me it was a choice but let me clear, for most people it is not a choice; it is the way they *are,* period, end of story—regardless, it doesn't matter!) granted me an immediate belonging to a community. This was the first time in my life where I felt like I had a place, a grounding in the world. I wore my freedom rings, painted upside down pink triangles on the back pockets of my cut off shorts, and tromped around in Doc Martens like I invented homosexuality. The reason I took such pride (pun intended) in my affiliation with the gay community was because I was deeply grateful for feeling like a group of nice people accepted me as their own.

I relished being a Friend of Dorothy and being viewed as a cool representative of "the family."[xiv] In fact, that is what we called ourselves, family. This is no small detail because many of the people that I knew had been disowned by their families or at best, begrudgingly tolerated by them. So to have a family—of any sort— was a bond that kept so many of us disparate souls together as a community.

I was called a "lipstick lesbian" because I had long hair, wore makeup and had an eclectic but feminine style. My girlfriend was an African-American lipstick lesbian. Being a lipstick lesbian had a special status back then because they were considered more of a rarity and turned the whole diesel dyke stereotype on its head. So not only was I a welcomed part of this family, but I was a distinguished representative by standards of that day.

Societal Discrimination

I think that one of the chief unifiers of our gay community in college was the fact that societally we were still underdogs. The position of being threatened by the world at large kept us galvanized. A common mission vacuum seals a group of people. Discrimination fortified the mission rather than weakened it.

Growing up as a white, middle-class, healthy female, I had no outward signs that would elicit discrimination in public. The Rainbow Experience erased such immunity. It was one of the best things to ever happen to me.

I learned many behavioral adjustments while navigating an intolerant world: How to speak in code to assess if I was speaking to a gay-friendly person or not. ("Are you family?" or "Are you a Friend of Dorothy?") Hold hands with my girlfriend out of view. Pretend that I was only friends with someone I was dating. Ignore hateful stares. Walk rapidly to my car and quickly lock the doors once inside. Use ambiguous language when speaking to someone who you know won't approve but neither do you want to betray your own truth. Contain anger when a straight male would immediately make my girlfriend and me a subject of his projected sexual fantasies, like we were toys for his amusement rather than real human beings.

These behavioral modifications were just the dressing on the wound. The deeper revelation was the awareness of hate that lurks like an invisible, insidious fog in a world that appears fine and normal until it gets provoked by something the status quo fears.

Pain Behind the Stereotypes

Why is it that wounded people often have the greatest sense of humor? I noticed that the gay community in college actually embraced some of the funny stereotypes and didn't take itself too seriously in that regard. But behind the caricatures of lesbians in Dockers and Birkenstocks who own multiple cats and drive Subarus or gay men who sashay, talk with a lisp and love Judy Garland were, get this, real humans!

I observed so many women and men who had come from tragic backgrounds often fraught with sexual abuse and domestic violence. These childhood experiences often seemed to be the impetus for many young women to experiment with lesbianism. I myself was a prime example. This was the only family or social system that I had experienced in which males were non-threatening.

There were also young women and men who were just born gay. Period. And during that time, being born gay came with its own host of problems. So many people I knew had stories of heartbreak, isolation, and sadness. The collective pain almost overwhelmed me at times.

Had I never experienced this lifestyle and community from the inside, I would have only known these people as *those* people, as otherness, as a foreign idea. I saw up close and personal the humanity behind the labels.

Compassion
Rumi is attributed to saying, "The wound is where the light enters."

Living as a gay woman for a few years in college, allowed me to see and experience life from the perspective of a group of people who otherwise were universally denied, castigated, shamed and marginalized in our culture. Behind all the rhetoric swirling around the LGBTQ community—homophobic vitriol and ignor-ance on one side and pleas, protests, and demonstrations on the other—were simply humans who wanted to love and be loved and have a recognized place and purpose in this world.

On a larger scale, this made me consider other individuals or groups of people who experience marginalization in our country or simply suffer unnoticeably. It took me several years for the gravity of this revelation to sink in. Eventually though, no longer did I assume I knew what it was like to be someone else and therefore make value judgments about them.

One Human Family
The ubiquity of pain and suffering coupled with the longing for love and belonging is the common thread of all humans, regardless of race, gender, sexual orientation, socio-economic

status, religion, or whether you are a cat or dog person. We are inextricably woven together.

This awareness, that now runs marrow deep in my being, was well worth any perceived loss or injustice previously inflicted upon me. Being coerced into quitting ballet, being scorned from the church, being treated as an object, which ultimately led me to the gay community, all of that was worth realizing who my true family is—the human family.

Confession #5: The Church: Your Tribe is not My Vibe

You may wonder why I have the category of The Church under beliefs. From a theological perspective, Ecclesiology is the study of the role of The Church proper, as a universal construct within Christianity. It essentially refers to the belief that the people of Christianity, as embodied by the universal church, have about themselves and their mission as an institution.

It is worth a sidebar acknowledgment that I am speaking in general terms and there are always exquisite exceptions—singular churches that embody love and compassion—to the bombs that I'm about to drop. I am, after all, writing about the broader American Church that has caused mass defection from Christianity.

Let me start by painting a picture for you. If you're not from the South or a rural or suburban enclave, just hang on to your hat and use your imagination.

You know you are in God's country when the cars have silver fishes on their rear bumper and highway billboards ominously warn of Armageddon. The women wear tight t-shirts with bedazzled crosses and hang a medley of wooden crosses (purchased at Hobby Lobby) somewhere in their kitchen or living room. Local businesses name themselves things like Higher Power Electrical or In His Steps Plumbing and Heating. Little boys play in Christian sports leagues and learn to point to the sky thanking God for their wins. Little girls attend Christian dance studios where they are never taught to move their hips and they perform to sanitized versions of secular songs on the radio. (If you haven't heard "Chosen Ladies" to the tune of Beyonce's "Single Ladies" or

"JesusBack" to the tune of "SexyBack" by Justin Timberlake, then you haven't lived.)

These ideological terrariums are a suffocating environment for anything foreign to their ways of thinking, doing or being, much like when Spongebob Squarepants visits Sandy in her underwater, air-filled dome and nearly dehydrates to death.

You are either in. Or you are out. And when you are out, you are O.U.T.

I had several female Christian "friends" from Megachurchland during my second marriage. Our daughters played together and attended the same conservative Christian private school. Those ladies did not know of the abuse I endured with my second husband until I finally had the courage to leave him. Suddenly, I was no longer in their club. My ex-husband did a remarkable job of "speaking Jesus" and that was more impressive to these ladies than the reality that hid behind his manipulative words.

My children and I were homeless for nearly three months after I left him. He continued to live in our 3800-square-foot house and party with sorority girls while the children and I piecemealed our existence together. I had run out of money and had nowhere to go. My Christian friends weren't interested in our plight. A kind Jewish family that I barely knew took me, my three children, and our cat into their home while I waited for legal intervention.

This experience paints the stark reality of what has happened to the American church. It has become nothing short of a masquerade for tribalism. And tribalism is about protecting self-interests at the expense of the greater whole and often the greater good. This is *not* Love.

After being shunned and forgotten by my evangelical Christian friends post-marriage, I decided to return to my progressive seminary and finish the master's degree that I had started 12 years earlier before I ever got married. I reasoned that the problem was *evangelical* Christianity and anticipated a fresh welcome by those in Methodism.

The seminary itself has to be one of the most inclusive and embracing places on the planet as far as I'm concerned.

Simultaneously, I became very involved in one of the largest Methodist churches in the country. As a newly single mom, I had decided I would pursue a career as a Methodist minister. I loved God, I loved people and I understood suffering and metaphorical resurrection. My own life was living proof.

In order to become an ordained minister in the Methodist church, you have to begin by meeting with a committee at your home church. Methodists love committees. The composition of this committee includes a few ministers and a few laypeople who are charged with evaluating your fitness for ministry before recommending you for ordination. The process can take a few years. A notable person on my particular committee was one of the very first female ministers to have been ordained in the Methodist church many years earlier. While I 100% support the process of vetting candidates, I was not expecting how this ship would go down.

I showed up at the church for my very first—and what would be my last—interview with this committee. I wore a cream-colored boatneck sweater with puffy sleeves, pearls, gray slacks and heels. Professional attire by any standards.

When I got to the meeting room, there was another young woman awaiting her turn to meet with the committee. She looked like she had just scattered seed for her backyard chickens after having milked the goats after having serenaded her livestock with the soothing acoustic sounds of a John Denver song. Her dreads went down to her waist, her patchwork prairie skirt barely hiding the Birkenstocks that exposed her bare feet.

While I totally dig the hippie thing, I thought to myself, "Man, that sure isn't a professional way to present yourself," for what was essentially a job interview.

My turn came with the committee. I sat at one end of the large table, the members of the committee around the table and the chair of the committee opposite me. The chairperson was a male minister who had been on staff for quite some time. He started out gently asking me why I was interested in ministry. I explained that ever since I was a little girl my greatest passion was the pursuit of God. I shared some about my abusive childhood and recent marriage, illustrating that only the power of God could resurrect me to a place where I now knew Peace, Joy, and infinite Love. I wanted to serve and help others experience their own personal transformations. The chair, let's call him Steve, cocks his head back, cups his hand to his chin, tapping a finger over his mouth while raising one of his bushy eyebrows. The warm fuzzies I had brought to the interview began to drain the room like cold, day-old, dirty bath water.

"So basically," he sighs, "you were abused as a child and have three kids from two marriages. You are a failure at marriage and parenting. How are you possibly qualified to minister to others?"

The room closed in on me like it does when you are about to faint, my breath temporarily suspended.

With a measured cadence, my words pierced the room, "*That* is exactly what qualifies me to minister to others."

I let those words hang in awkward silence, my eyes fixed on his. Someone shuffled papers to look busy. Eventually, Steve gathered his senses like someone does after they had just been slapped. He concluded my interview saying I could check back with them in a year.

Alrighty then, I thought to myself as I left the room. Hippie girl sauntered in after me with virtual daisies swirling about her like a Snapchat filter. I thought to myself, "Good luck, girl."

Interesting postscript to this anecdote—hippie girl went on to not only be ordained but to be a force in advocating for social justice issues in our city. I have the deepest respect for her and her work. Unlike me though, she had a lengthy Methodist pedigree and is married to another Methodist minister.

Annnd the committee felt the need to get one more last word in. The elder female minister who had been at the meeting caught me in the parking lot a few days later and told me, "Rachel, the committee thinks your sweater was a little tight."

I clearly wasn't going to fit in that tribe either. This experience and others with this progressive Christian church just proved that tribalism comes in different shades and forms but it is tribalism nonetheless. It shocked me to no end that this church didn't understand the concept that a person's life, resurrected from living death into living Love, is precisely what the story of Jesus is about. But I didn't fit their mold of a pedigreed past so I was not good enough for them or their church.

I don't share these stories to make it about me. And I most certainly am not trying to paint a picture that I was a victim in these circumstances. Rather, in the spirit of truth, I am holding a mirror up for the American Church to view themselves, should they be willing to look. The American Church wouldn't be hemorrhaging adherents if they were doing things right.

Tribalism plays out in churches today in at least two primary ways. Firstly, like me as a heterosexual girl in college finding a sense of belonging in the gay community, everyday people are allured and captured by communities that give them a strong identity and a sense of importance. People do this *despite fundamental ideological differences* with the church, like I was able to convince myself that I was gay for a few years. That's how powerful the need for belonging is.

I can't tell you how many people I know who have attended homophobic churches but personally have gay friends and think that they should have equal legal rights. Yet, they attend places such as Watershark citing reasons like the pastor is hip and inspirational or there's a great worship band. Their individual compulsion to belong to a spiritual tribe overpowers the truth that they know otherwise. This applies to a host of social issues: gender equality, domestic abuse and more.

But please, for the love of your gay hairdresser and all things RuPaul, could you quit supporting these outposts of bigotry that disguise themselves as havens of holiness?

Secondly, tribalism is fortified by the church itself. Like I mentioned in The Rainbow Experience, tribes galvanize when there is a perceived threat from the outside. Sometimes there is a legitimate threat, sometimes there is not. The American Church perceives there to be a threat from an increasingly secular culture, which the church thinks is the reason they are suffering attrition.

News flash: the attrition is the result, not the reason.

The reason the Church is experiencing attrition faster than Donald Trump blame-shifts is because it is more concerned with preserving itself than evolving to become relevant in 21st-century America. The real threat to the American Church is extinction—not the secular culture rejecting it. And they are trying to avoid extinction by serving up the same dogma and exclusionism that is causing their very demise. It is like the church is gnawing off its own arm. *If we keep feeding ourselves to ourselves, then eventually we will grow again*, is the thinking.

The first step in solving a problem is recognizing that you have one. And Church, you have a problem.

Confession #6: The Dark Side: Satan, Sin, Hell, & Evil

I'm going to keep this one short and sweet.

Satan Is the Personification of Evil
Satan is the anthropomorphic version of evil in the same way that God, as an external-otherness deity floating in the sky, is an anthropomorphic version of a creator, mostly benevolent god. There is no red-costumed Archenemy prowling around with a pitchfork ready to strike you at his whims. This character is an ancient way of explaining evil in the world.

Fear Sources Evil and Is the Counterforce to Love
There is not a *being* that lurks around but there is a force, originating in our egoic minds, that seeks to destroy us. At its basest level, this force is Fear. Just listen to your negative self-talk for one day and there it is. It can operate on an individual, collective or systemic level. When you gather a group of fear-based minds, then mass evil can occur. This counterforce to Love does the opposite of what Love does: it divides, weakens, and kills.

Sin Is the Manifestation of the Absence of Love
I do not care for the word "sin" because it has become laden with antiquated meanings and shame that serve no positive purpose in cultivating a healthy, spiritually vibrant person. I prefer to be obsessed with Love and remain aware when I am without it so that I may return to Love.

However, the legitimate concept behind the word *sin* is worth attention. With this frame of reference, this condition is when we think, speak or behave out of Fear. I know I am mixing languages here, but I love the definition of *sin* in Spanish, which means 'without.' When we are without Love, we "sin." Trying to categorize sins in lesser or greater degrees is a slippery slope and a descent I'd rather not entertain.

Hell Is Living in the Absence of Love

We create our own hell. Period. For anyone who you hope will rot there one day, chances are they are already rotting on the inside in some way. And chances are, you are too if that person still has that much power over you.

Confession #7: The Force: Salvation & Heaven

I rode a bus every day to and from middle school. During the 30-minute ride home, I would often gab and be silly with other kids trying to act cool, all the while feeling horribly uncool and unworthy. I don't think I was alone in my feelings of low self-worth—it seems to be a rite of passage in middle school. We were all testing our bravado and boundaries. Boys picked on other boys and teased the girls. Girls pretended to be annoyed with the boys and would randomly exert passive-aggression toward other girls. Super fun times!

Out of all the middle-school antics that I remember from those years, the very worst thing ever to occur on that bus was enacted by me.

Another girl named Alicia, who was in my grade, was on the same bus route. I envied her clothes because her parents bought her Forenza and Espirit and she had Swatch watches, the pinnacle middle-school status piece. I wore hand-me-downs from older kids in our church. She kept mostly to herself but seemed so put together and self-assured. I wanted what she seemed to have.

There was something else that was different about Alicia. She was Jewish.

To be Jewish in my Louisiana hometown was as rare as a Baptist in a liquor store. Jewish folks were viewed as an odd curiosity but mostly with sanctimonious disdain. To add to this cultural climate of ignorance and arrogance, my church taught that we had the distinctive duty to witness to Jews. I had been eyeing Alicia for months, not only because of her coveted wardrobe but because I had been trained to believe I was obligated to convert her. I had an internal battle waging inside of me because something kept holding me back from reaching out to her about Jesus. Yet at the same time I "knew" it was my divine responsibility.

Finally, one afternoon on the bus ride home, I garnered the (imagined) gumption of God. Pivoting around in my seat, I confronted her. We had the close proximity and attention of the other kids around us.

"Alicia, do you believe in Jesus?" I asked, knowing that I set her up with a no-win scenario.

Her eyes widened as if she had just seen an apparition, her face turning bright red as she sat upright and back in her seat. Clutching her books to her chest she muttered, "I believe he was a good man..."

"Don't you ever worry about your salvation?" I drilled deeper.

Alicia was rightfully feeling cornered. Other kids were fixed on our conversation. I was telling myself that I was a local hero for taking on this battle.

She responded in a weakened tone something along the lines that she was Jewish and she didn't really know what I was talking about.

I had run out of God-gumption because I didn't know what I was talking about either. So I just sighed a huge "Hmphhff!" and rotated back in my seat. "At least I tried," I told myself.

In retrospect, I was an idiot and a bully. Alicia, you were grace under fire. Middle school is hard enough without pompous little shits like me making it worse. Please forgive me for making a scene at your expense and for imposing my ill-guided beliefs on you. I am sorry that I disrespected you. And please forgive my envy of your clothes. I hope happiness was with you then and is with you now.

What exactly is it that we are to be saved from? And why do we need to be saved?

You will get different answers depending on what type of Christian you ask but the answers are typically something like this: Humans need saving from their original sinful nature (the "what"). Humans need to recognize Jesus Christ as the one and only way to God so that we can live in heaven after we die (the "how" and the "why").

This construction has reduced the idea of salvation to nothing more than a membership card to the Christian tribe, particularly amongst evangelicals. Case in point: Have you ever known anyone who has been saved multiple times? It doesn't matter what kind of deplorable life they live in between salvations. It's just a matter of asking for forgiveness and claiming to believe the correct doctrine about Jesus and *presto!* they are back in the club! Haven't we all known folks who have been Born Again Again Again Again Again (BAAAAA, like a biblical sheep)?

The spiritual aim of salvation, as it should be, is for us to have union with God. I'm referring to God as Love. One can only have union with Love when we learn to differentiate our egoic minds from Love and choose Love. In this sense, we are being "saved" from our sinful nature (meaning, without Love) and the old self dies and a new self is born.

Salvation started for me when I was brave enough to reject the outmoded and ineffective interpretation of salvation and accept the truth about reality, which began with facing myself. It did not involve the mere recitation of a "sinner's prayer," assertion of a doctrine about Jesus as God, or going to church every Sunday.

Rather, through deep spiritual work, I surrendered my Ego and opened my being to a power greater than me. As spiritual awareness expanded, my thoughts and behaviors refined. After steadfast discipline, I found myself in a state of Peace, Love and Joy that transcends circumstances and the whims or judgments of others.

That is what I call heaven.

The Dovetail: Parting Thoughts, Summations, and a Send-Off

We're Not in Kansas Anymore...

Judy Garland and *The Wizard of Oz* were revered icons for the gay community particularly in the mid-to-late 20th century. There are a few posited explanations. Gay men during and after World War II saw Garland as a symbol of the drama that they themselves experienced living a suppressed life, fraught with alcohol, drugs, and relationship mayhem. She was a common persona for drag shows. The character of Dorothy, played by Garland, is accepting of those who are different and boy, did gay men know they were different during that time in history. The movie itself carries symbolism for the gay community's desire to break free from a black-and-white world and experience Technicolor living in a world that would embrace them as they were.

The term "Friends of Dorothy" originated during the Second World War so that gay servicemen could identify one another without exposure or incrimination. The powerful drive toward authenticity is unceasing. People die on the inside when they live incongruently with the truth of their being. Society can fight what is real and true but one way or the other, truth prevails or the entire societal structure will eventually fail.

Thankfully for the gay community, much progress has been made in their rightful struggle for equality. We are still far from the destination, though, legally and culturally. Revolutionizing religion is of paramount importance in recognizing the LGBTQ community as sacred individuals. I am grateful that my personal experience and academic study has emboldened me to appreciate the plight and support the fight for our gay brothers and sisters.

Much in the same way, I hope that emerging American Nones will find liberation in rejecting the beliefs that are errant in modern Christianity and reclaim their own spiritual journey. It is my greatest passion to encourage and support this spiritual revolution.

On Beliefs and One Great Big Tribe

In this chapter, I have delineated some of the common Christian beliefs that ceased to be effective for my spiritual development. I have suggested alternative ways of viewing these beliefs or unilateral replacements of them.

In the Information Age, we no longer need to rely on ancient, cryptic analogies to explore deep meanings. While some people may still find inspiration in stories about camels and wineskins, for example, a growing number of people would benefit better by getting straight to the truth behind them (if there is any) so that they can immediately begin creating better lives for themselves. This allows us to live in rational authenticity while cultivating a rewarding spiritual life.

However, lest we become a version of the very arrogant thing that has repelled us from modern Christianity, we must keep our focus on Love for all people. The bottom line is, it does not matter if you believe that Jesus literally rose from the dead or if heaven is an actual destination after we die—*if* Love undergirds your doctrines and dictates your attitudes, thoughts, and behaviors. I know countless people from various religions who believe doctrines that are sheerly fantastical to me. Yet these friends of mine are informed and guided by Love and their lives reflect that in their generous, gracious, and embracing ways.

For those of us who cannot extend ourselves for such doctrines, we must focus our belief in Love and live our lives by that measure. Part of the demonstration of that Love is to embrace loving religious people who may believe things that seem absurd to us. Also, in the spirit of truth and Love, we must refuse to enable those who abuse the power of the church or the influence of religion.

If we create a spiritual climate where people are free to explore that which actually transforms their lives for the better, then the reality of our One Human Family will be actualized despite our differences.

The World is our Tribe.

Believe in Love.

I Feel Like Dancing

I may not have become a professional dancer but I haven't stopped dancing! I'm the kind of person who dances down the bread aisle at the grocery store, embarrasses my kids at sporting events when time-out music is played, and owns my own portable, illuminated disco globe for impromptu family dance-offs.

Joy moves me to dance and dancing grows my joy!

Spontaneous dancing is something I do that keeps my spirit lit. Let's check the spiritual "litness" of some common religious practices in Chapter Four.

CHAPTER 4

PRACTICES

Don't believe the smiles. This photo was taken in Georgia before we began our trek back to Louisiana. This may have been right before the barn incident. Or even right after it. I was that practiced in faking smiles in order to escape further beatings.

Opener: Have You Driven a Ford... Lately?

What do an industrial-sized mustard jar, flagellation in a barn, and a prison break all have in common?

A Ford Econoline van of course.

When my family would go on the 11-hour road trip to the Middle of Nowhere, Georgia to visit my stepdad's parents, he would not stop for anything or anyone unless *he* needed to pee, which was practically never. The rest of us had to squat in the back of the van and relieve ourselves in a mustard jar. I often wondered if he enjoyed humiliating us like that.

One time at the tail end of our visit to the Middle of Nowhere, after we had packed up and were about to hit the road, the van was parked on a downhill slope. I attempted to shut the sliding door but gravity took over and slammed it. My stepdad took that as an act of defiance- that I "slammed" a door- so he promptly marched me down the hill, across a pasture, and into a barn. I was forced to hang on to the cross beams of the barn wall where he beat me with his belt. The posture I assumed was more debasing than the beating itself. After all, I was used to beatings.

The visits to Georgia were pretty unbearable but paled in comparison to the life that awaited us once we returned home. By age 14, my mother and stepfather had decided to homeschool my brother and me. In reality, it was a house arrest.

There was little time for actual education. (This is actually a good thing because according to them the earth was 4,000 years old and dinosaurs were a hoax.) The overriding majority of my waking hours centered on how efficiently to wash and fold laundry, iron clothes, make beds, clean toilets, wash dishes, cook dinner, make 2am bottles, change diapers, dust furniture, polish furniture, mop floors, vacuum floors, wipe baseboards, clean windows, pick up dog poop, weed flower gardens, care for my three younger brothers, and go grocery shopping. (Exhale.)

Which brings me back to the Ford Econoline. That lumbering bad boy was my ticket to pockets of freedom every time I went to the grocery store. You see, I learned how to drive when I was 14. I was a 90-pound waif behind the wheel of a bus. It wasn't the coolest ride in town but I rocked it anyway perched up in that bucket seat with a perm wild enough to make you think I had drained the town of its electricity. Driving the van gave me a sense of autonomy and liberation from the prison at home.

So was the Ford Econoline a reminder of humiliation and debasement or a symbol for escape?

It was neither, both, and more.

Menu and Music: Carbs and Cars

Bread gets a bad rep these days. Carbs, carbs, carbs. Well, ancient people weren't concerned about carbs and bread became a featured element in what is arguably the most sacred Christian ritual. So as an homage to the sacrament of "The Lord's Supper," as we called it in the South, bread is our menu item for the chapter on practices.

This particular recipe is what my children affectionately call "church bread." When I was a single mom and had returned to seminary, I baked this bread every Saturday to be used for communion the following day. The recipe was given to me by the presiding minister of that service, of whom I have the greatest respect as a human and clergyman.

Granted, refined carbs are not optimal. But everything in moderation, grasshopper!

The body needs carbs and people need rituals and traditions—even those who say they don't. Rock along with The Cars, and "let's go" on a journey together making pit stops along the way to inspect some common Christian practices.

The Backstory: Take Me Away

The Econoline van was a vehicle and an instrument. Like anything, it can be used for good, bad or indifferent purposes. Also, like anything, it has a meaning that I choose to give to it.

I have many thoughts about that van. It can be viewed as a symbol of oppression and violence from my childhood. It was also a foreshadowing of resilience because the very thing that was an instigator of inflicted pain, I later mastered when I learned to drive. At which point it became a symbol of escape.

However, the reality is the van itself was benign. After all, it was not what actually harmed me. The human agency behind the appropriation of the van was the true source of wrongdoing, as it always is. Further, the sense of freedom I had when I drove the van began within me. I did not know it then but the internal empowerment over oppression was sourced from the power of God as Love, a Greater-Than Knowing that there was life available outside of my personal hell. It had nothing to do with the van. The van was, again, merely a vehicle.

I can also reflect on that van with gratitude. It was air conditioned and was a safe vehicle on the roads. And at least riding in that van was a heck of a lot better than if we had lived 150 years ago and would have been in a covered wagon. Yes, sometimes you have to dig deep but there is always a reason for gratitude. In this sense, the van represents an opportunity for me to expand spiritually, even when circumstances are dire, by choosing to allow something to make me better, not bitter.

Here's the thing—rituals and traditions are themselves benign just like the van. They only have the value that are ascribed to them. In the best use of religious practices, they should be a tangible exercise or expression that unites our transcendent, spiritual nature with the mundane world. They are meant to impart meaning and transport the practitioner to a more evolved state of being. And they serve as a concrete reminder of how we should live our lives.

Such practices are inextricably bound with our beliefs because the latter yields the former causing an infinite loop in which one fortifies the other. This relation cuts both ways because the more you believe something, the more valuable the practice becomes and the less you believe something, the less valuable the practice becomes.

This truth became glaringly apparent to me when I used to make the "church" bread for communion. The parishioner experienced something like this:

The setting was a beautiful French Gothic chapel that was quite large by chapel standards. The liturgical service was elevated by the soaring sounds of a pipe organ and enveloped by the mottled hues of arched stained glass windows. Two long rows of wooden pews flanked a processional aisle that led to the chancel. The chancel had a lectern, pulpit, and an altar that held the communion elements. The otherwise nondescript rear wall bore a simple brass cross and had a stained glass Rose Window poised atop. An altar rail suggested a demarcation between the human and the holy, dividing the congregation from the goings-on of the chancel.

This altar rail is also where communion took place. After a formal service of prayers, lectionary readings, a sermon, and recitation of the Apostle's Creed, the minister would invoke the Holy Spirit and bless the bread and grape juice. (Most Protestant groups don't actually use wine.) Congregants would kneel at the rail and offer their open hands to receive the elements. One worship leader would break off a piece of bread and say to the person being served something like, "The body of Christ broken for you." Following behind would be a second worship leader who would say, "The blood of Christ poured out for you" while offering a chalice of juice. The congregant would then dip the bread in the chalice and consume it. Some people would choose to linger at the rail and say private prayers before returning to their seats. The service would come to a swift conclusion with the benediction.

Here is what the parishioner didn't know or likely never thought about:

On the day before, when I was at home baking the communion bread, I was likely stressed to the gills. I had been at work the better part of the day, feeling guilty for not being home with my young children. I likely had a good cry about not being able to pay my bills and my ex-husband had probably recently threatened me in some way.

Baking the bread was a form of meditation through the squall of single motherhood. Every time I kneaded the dough, I folded some of my hurts, hopes, and disappointments into it as a way of letting go. By the time I shaped it into its final dome form, it was as if I were choosing to package and put away another micro-chapter of my life that seemed beyond my control. The baking process simply fortified that personal resolution.

Sunday would come and I was running on fumes, exhausted from the week before and from staying up late to prepare the adult Sunday School lesson that I would teach that morning. Getting my children ready and willing to go to church was like waging an apocalyptic war. Interestingly, the promise of being able to finish off the leftover communion bread after the service was the only way to get them out the door.

Before the service began, those of us who worked on the chancel would be in the back room putting on our albs and making jokes that weren't chancel appropriate. They weren't distasteful—just not proper enough for high church. We'd get all mic'd up and then run to the rear of the chapel and assume our church dispositions before proceeding into the chapel. The service would go off without a hitch, congregants would participate in communion, and afterwards, the chapel would empty quickly as the organ bellowed on.

The worship crew would convene in the back room again, this time taking off the albs and ropes. The leftover bread would be a mangled heap inside a Ziploc bag. It always struck me as odd how the bread that had been an instrument of meditation for me the day before, then sacredly used in a ritual for dozens of soul searching people, suddenly seemed insignificant and forgettable, much like how our animated selves ultimately are reduced to an empty lump of mass upon death.

The official way to dispose of Eucharistic elements is for them to be "reverentially consumed" immediately after the service or to be "returned to the earth." I'm not so sure how reverent we ever were, but my kids had a blast either throwing crumbs to the crows or shoveling wads of doughy carbs into their little mouths over the course of Sunday afternoons.

The purpose of this story is not to relate my personal woes to a Christian ritual. Rather, what I love about it is that the pinnacle feature of the church service—communion—began and ended with the most basic of human qualities. The bread was made with intention to release a sense of hardship and convert that energy into something that would hopefully bless others. The inflation of the value of that bread occurred during a religious ritual that elevated the spirits of many people, if only for a fleeting moment. Later, it was rabidly consumed by temperamental kiddos.

Religious practices are human created, human executed, and human interpreted.

Growing up in the cult, a vast amount of Christian practices were ignored or unknown altogether. The few that they did observe, communion being one of them, was done with a superficial understanding of its meaning. The Christian practices I experienced growing up were parallel to the beliefs that I was taught. They were simply flat assumptions that you were supposed to blindly accept in order to be a member of the tribe.

It was not until I had spent a decade as an agnostic in my early adulthood and then landed at a progressive seminary that I was exposed to the elegance and depth of Christian rituals and traditions. This is where I first learned about the vast Church Calendar, liturgy, creeds, iconography, the symbolism of church accoutrements and architecture, and the history and meaning of the full array of Christian practices. Several years and substantial student loan debt later, I developed a deep respect and appreciation for what these things ultimately represented.

That precisely highlights the problem regarding the current state of religious practices today. The *meaning* behind nearly all of these practices exist to address the omnipresent issues of the human condition. But the *vehicles* in which these meanings are imparted, vis a vis antiquated religious practices, have plummeted in relevance and relatability in a 21st-century world. The meanings are relevant. The practices have become increasingly less so, ceasing to be transformational tools for a better life.

In this chapter, I will explore several rituals or traditions— some that are familiar and some that may not be. In each section, I will state the commonly understood meaning or purpose of the practice. Next, I will contrast how it is experienced by many people in modern American Christianity. Lastly, I will share what I have come to believe is the meaning behind the ritual and how I have made that intended meaning relevant in my own life, challenging you to do the same.

Confessions

Confession #1: Going to Church

Commonly Believed Purpose
The Church proclaims that we should attend services to worship God, experience community, and further spiritual development.

Reality Check
The overwhelming majority of people don't go to church. The Pew Research Center cites that as of 2014, 37% of Americans report going to services weekly. This leaves over 60% of the country attending only a handful of times per year or not at all. There is even a special moniker for those who attend only during Christmas and Easter— "Chreasters."

I recommend that you conduct a casual poll of those in your personal circle. Chances are, most of you rarely if ever attend a church service. Baby boomers and women are more likely to attend church than subsequent generations and men respectively. And with each subsequent, younger generation, church attendance dramatically diminishes for both men and women.

For folks under the age of 50, I have observed a very common scenario. Two people got married and had kids. They think going to church will make both them and their kids better people. Fast forward 20 years and they have since quit going to church when their kids rebelled about it in middle school. They are now going through a divorce. The dad feels free from living a religiously sham life and the mom returns to church in hopes of filling the hole in her soul.

This dynamic is based on the external-otherness God and keeps people chasing a dangling holy carrot. Increasingly, more Americans are tired of running on this treadmill to nowhere. Let's contrast the commonly lauded purposes of church attendance with why they don't hold up in the court of public practice anymore.

Firstly, worshipping God is an outmoded way of understanding what God is. The more I have learned about the evolution of theology and religious practices, the more absurd it became to worship a God "out there" by singing his praises and telling him how great he is. This abstraction is merely a reflection of the external-otherness, egocentric, human-proxy God that I refuse to believe in. Personally, I feel silly singing songs of praise to a human-made construction of a God deity. If congregants would take all of the energy that they use hurling flattery toward a fictitious God, and instead redirect it toward recognizing the Love in others then my-oh-my, what a difference it would make in this world.

Additionally, a 2018 Pew Report states that, of the Americans who actually do attend services, the overwhelming reason is that they want to feel close to God. On the surface, this may sound reasonable. But check this out:

Going to church out of necessity to feel close to God is like falling prey to religious capitalism. It is similar to The Scarcity Principle of free enterprise economics. Many popular brands have built revenue generating monsters based on this. Apple created the iPad that in turn created the demand for the iPad, a type of product consumers never knew they "needed." Apple controls the accessibility of iPads to the vociferous public who wants them. Therefore, Apple engineers both the demand and the supply, leaving a constant tension of scarcity in the marketplace. This serves to drive up their own profits.

Churches do this too. In effect, the perception of the scarcity of God is perpetuated by the Church. Whether explicit or implicit, the message communicated is that the physical church—and its respective affiliated denomination—is *the place* where one can most assuredly, most tangibly feel close to God. Churches are competing for your attendance and money so that they can survive, now more than ever.

There is nothing wrong with going to church. But it is grievous to me that the Church perpetuates a mythos that the building is the preeminent place to be close to God and that people, who are otherwise parched for connection to the divine, don't know any different. This construction is another example of an outmoded concept of God. If we change the way we understand God, we can change the way we experience God.

Secondly, the church is supposed to be a place for community or "Christian fellowship." As I pointed out in the previous chapter, by and large, modern church functions more as a tribal identifier. The grim truth is that many churches have become self-sustaining islands within a broader, *real* community. It's like *The Village* by M. Night Shyamalan in which a group of people, initially for decent reason, removed themselves from the rest of the world and built a wall to keep others out and themselves in. They tell themselves it is better that way—isolated from the broader world based on self-righteous principles. The problem is, eventually people learn to explore past the wall. The power of nature, that is fueled by the power of Love, demands to be known. And real community includes *everyone,* even those beyond the wall.

Lastly, for reasons I've previously stated, a vast majority of the American public no longer view the institutional church as a viable source for spiritual development. The church loves to place this blame on the public, citing a sinful, secularization of the masses. I will always maintain that if your model, Church, actually worked, then people wouldn't be leaving faster than bats fleeing an Ozzy Osbourne concert. Besides, there's some stiff competition for church these days.

Consider the rise of yoga practice and indoor cycling classes as a worship service replacement. More faithful than most Christians, women will slide into their leggings, roll up their mats or grab their cycle shoes, and swish their ponytails right into a class. Here they benefit from a sweaty workout, positive messaging, and strong community all in one hour. BOOM.

By and large, church attendance as personal practice is already an antiquated thing of the past just like the belief system that goes hand-in-hand with it. This is evidenced by the innumerable church buildings that are being sold and repurposed as community centers, music venues, art galleries, or breweries.

A trend in progressive Protestantism is to "reinvent" church by creating outpost-churches in coffee shops, youth community centers, and other forms of public commerce locations. The idea here is to meet people where they are. The problem that I have with this model is that there is still the undercurrent ambition to convert people to a doctrinal belief system.

A New View

Every day, every moment, go to church.

The world is your church. How you live your life is your worship.

Living should be an outpouring of Love. Recognize the divinity in others, even those you dislike the most, and be an extension of Love in your thoughts, words, and deeds.

Find your authentic community with the real people who make up your real community. Don't be afraid of those who are different from you. Stay connected to people. Forget about arbitrary, self-imposed boundaries that separate us from others.

Confession #2: Reading the Bible

Commonly Believed Purpose

Reading the Bible should be a ritualistic, daily devotional practice so that the practitioner can ingest the Word of God, furthering his or her spiritual development and obedience to God.

Reality Check

Considering the primacy that modern evangelical Christians place on reading the Bible in order to be in good standing with their ilk, one would assume that this is a deeply entrenched value in the history of the religion. But, there's a teeny, tiny problem.

There was no such thing as printed Bibles available to the public until a few hundred years ago and only the wealthy or academically elite had access to them. Even after printed Bibles became more available to the American public in the 19th century, there were still glaring discrepancies of literacy rates and educational opportunities along the race and gender divide.

The point being, it is a modern invention to equate one's Bible reading with one's spiritual fitness. In fact, for nearly all of Christian history, it was only through going to church that people *heard* scripture. There is no coincidence to the fact that the more available the Bible became to everyday people, the more Christian denominations splintered and propagated like bunnies on Spring Break.

Why is this? I've already covered the complexities of the Bible in the previous chapter. So with that in mind, imagine what happens when this collection of books, the sacred and the scary parts, run amuck in the hands of people with or without formal theological education and with their own agendas and worldviews. Chaos ensues. Whether one agrees with the Catholic church or not, they at least have had a method to keep things fairly organized by comparison.

The fragmentation of Christianity, as it relates to different inter-pretations of the Bible, can also be seen on a smaller scale both within particular churches and amongst individuals because interpretations are like boogers. Everyone picks their own. At which point, we make a full, ironic circle. Reading the Bible has led to great division within Christianity and yet it is one of the hallmark merit badges that Protestants place upon people to earn their tribal membership.

When I was mired in my abusive marriage with Husband #2 and subsequently when I was barely surviving as a single mom, little would make me more angry than some pious, stay-at-home Christian mom who would offer me this advice: "You just need to get up an hour earlier every day and have your quiet time with the Lord so that you can read your Bible and pray."

I immediately envisioned myself taking the largest Bible I owned and whacking her over the head with it. Multiple times.

There is so much wrong with that advice. For starters, God is not my Lord. Can we please quit referring to Divine Truth with ancient, masculine, regal monikers? I had been abused by men my whole life. The last thing I needed to do was worship one. AND if your life is luxurious enough to lose another hour of sleep so that you can read the most complicated amalgamation of recorded literature on the planet, then why don't YOU get up two hours earlier and do my hour for me?

I truly came to believe that the pressure that many Christians place upon other people to go to church and read their Bibles was commensurate with their own insecurity about well, everything. Why are you so concerned with measuring my spirituality?

Another issue centers on a theological debate that rose to prominence since the Protestant Revolution. Today, evangelicals particularly love to boast that they aren't like Catholics who have ritualized practices. Evangelicals criticize the "works righteous-ness" associated with Catholics, with their rosary beads, Hail Marys, confessions, etc., and claim their "faith righteousness" is superior. They say that you shouldn't have to *do* anything to earn salvation, you simply have to believe the correct things.

Sorry, but I have to summon Pee-Wee Herman, "I know you are but what am I?" Evangelical Christianity needs to quit pointing fingers. They may not have rosary beads or confessionals. Rather, they have simply replaced imposed Catholic rituals for their own. I would argue that reading the Bible is chief on their list. If you don't *do* that, then you aren't legit. Even worse, your eternal salvation ultimately is in jeopardy. You become what you fear.

A New View
The merit behind the idea that a devoted follower of Christianity should read their Bible regularly is two-fold. The content that we choose to absorb into our being affects us. And, as humans, we require ongoing maintenance to stay on a healthy course.

In other words, it is a good intention to seek out elevating, inspiring messages that will further our personal and spiritual development. And, we should do this on a regular basis. For some people, that might mean reading the Bible. (If this is you, I just hope that some effort has been put into understanding the nature of the Bible and knowing its context.)

I quit being militant about reading devotionals, of any kind, several years ago. For one thing, I was often reading the Bible with an unclean heart. I would read it only thinking of my ex-husband and how *he* should be the person learning the lessons that I was reading.

Also, I found that when I was telling myself that I *had* to do something (and if you feel like you *have* to do something, it is likely out of Fear), then I was keeping myself in an endless loop of feelings of inadequacy, which precluded peace. Not to mention, such a demand on my time was not practical in the life that I was juggling.

Rather, as my internal nature began rapid transformation due to other internal spiritual practices, the people, circumstances and even the messages that entered my life were exponentially more positive and affirming.

Now, if I choose to take time to read a portion of the Bible, I bring with me an informed knowledge of the contextual literature that I am reading, an open heart to learn from the voices of human antiquity that reveal both the darkest of our nature and the lightest of divine Love, and a freedom knowing that I choose to read the Bible; I am not shamed into it.

Confession #3: Baptism

Commonly Believed Purpose
Baptism is a ritual whereby the old self dies and a new self is born into Christlikeness.

Reality Check
I've been baptized by the Grim Reaper. Twice. The first time was when I was a child. Our little cult gathered in a backyard swimming pool and the man who routinely berated and beat me (stepdad) performed the honors. The second time was at Megachurchland as a newly divorced single mom of one. My soon-to-be second ex-husband was there, an unbeknownst harbinger of an abusive marriage yet to come. Megachurchland is the same church that pressured me into that marriage, shamed me into enduring abuse, and rejected me once I finally left him.

The fact that I was baptized by an abusive person and later by an abusive institution raises a question that Christianity has long debated. Does the rite of baptism still "take" even if the administrator is not holy? In other words, if the minister is a wicked person, does the baptism itself still hold any power for the person being baptized?

The question behind the question is this: Does the ritual itself possess the power or is it merely a symbol of something intangible that is supposed to take place? Depending on which Christian you ask, you will get different answers.

Because I am an American None, I am not confined to a particular dogma so here goes: Let's return to the Ford Econoline of my youth. Like the van, the functional reality is that all rituals only have the meaning we give them and if used properly, should prompt us toward the intended aspirational goal of the ritual, whose net results always begin and end *within* the individual person.

You cannot dunk, sprinkle or pour your way into a new you. The modern American Church has not done us any favors by propagating the notion that baptism itself will suddenly fill the void in your soul, make you quit abusing drugs, cheating on your spouse, or cure whatever your personal demon is. Whether it has been intentional or not, American Christianity has packaged rituals such as baptism like products that are sold along with nebulous claims for results. This is, in part, why people eventually quit buying into it and abandon church or Christianity altogether. There is a disconnect with claims that are being made and people's actual experience.

I can't tell you how many infant baptisms I've observed where the entire congregation collectively vows to help raise the child in Christian love. And yet, after the baby's baptism you never see that family in church again nor does the congregation remember who they were. Such a baptism is a vanity baptism. The parents (usually the mother) insist on the baptism ceremony—complete with the white, frilly gown, photoshoot, and brunch—but nothing actually *changes* because of this theatrical staging.

Within most forms of American Christianity, children and adults are supposed to seriously consider their motives before deciding to get baptized. This is fine and dandy but the problem I have is that the emphasis is on making a decision to perform an outward act. I would love to change this narrative to emphasize a daily, sometimes moment-to-moment, decision to live in a constant state of transformation toward Love.

I do consider myself to be baptized in the spiritual sense. It involved choosing to walk through great darkness and pain with the resolute commitment to believe in Love, turn to Love, and be Love, even when there was no visible sign that anything would get better for me. In this sense, an old self died and a new self was born because I refused to let darkness defeat me.

A New View
Whether you've been baptized in a church or not, the question to consider is, *How has your life been transformed?*

That, after all, is what baptism is really about—a transformation away from a life of defeat, darkness, and Fear and toward a life of freedom, light, and Love. If these merely sound like hollow words on a page, I most humbly and lovingly suggest that great things await you, if you so desire them and are willing to live an internally disciplined spiritual life.

Confession #4: Testimonies

Commonly Believed Purpose
The sharing of a person's testimony of conversion to Christianity or "life with Christ" is seen as a way of praising God for his faithfulness.

Reality Check
Let's get real: testimonies are a rallying cry for believers and a marketing tool used to lure non-believers.

Depending on what Christian tradition you may be familiar with, this particular practice may seem obscure or even unknown. For me, growing up in the Pentecostal cult, testimonies happened like this:

The little three-person worship band would be up on stage jamming out some high energy praise song that had people clapping, swaying their hands in the air, and when the Spirit really moved, dancing. Yes, dancing in the aisles. There would be a hoe-down, throw-down smack dab in the middle of the church. Sometimes people would even hook arms and twirl around like they were at a square dance. It was lit.

The handmade sign above the stage read "Jesus is Lord," reminding us why we were all there. That was the only decor in this Home Depot aluminum building. What we lacked in aesthetic appointments was compensated by hell-on-wheels fervor.

Eventually, the band would give way to the lulling sound of a slow, quieter song that droned on and on with repetitive phrases like, "Hosanna, Hosanna." Regardless of the fact that nobody knew what Hosanna actually meant, the hypnotic mantra coupled with the melodic instruments effectively put people into a trance.

And then, out of the blue, as if someone got hit over the head like Little Bunny Foo Foo, a person would awaken out of the fog and then meekly approach the stage. The pastor, who took himself very seriously, would confer with this person and upon determining he had a legit word from God, walk with him to the microphone. This was the cue for the band to get even quieter, just enough to stoke the emotions in the room but not too much to overpower the speaker.

The slain-in-the-spirit disciple would then share an impromptu testimony of how God has recently worked in his life. It was a familiar refrain: I'm a wicked sinner and did X,Y, Z but God did A,B, C and now I am a *real* believer and God is mighty indeed!

Later in life during Marriage #2 and while attending an evangelical church, testimonies were carefully staged. In fact, they were often quite literally produced as a high-end video that would be shown during a service. It was typically the story of a husband and wife who had two cherubic kiddos but they were on the brink of divorce. Then, as a last-ditch effort, they signed up for the church's marriage seminar and *presto!*, they are happily married again. Or, it was the story of a person who was battling cancer, who previously had lapsed in their Christian faith but returned during their medical plight. And praise Jesus, after getting serious about God, the cancer went POOF.

Here's the testimony I always wanted to hear: Where was God when you actually got divorced or you knew you were going to die from cancer? Or, how about a testimony in which you discovered you *weren't* a wretched piece of pond scum?

The problem I have with testimonies is that they are used to bait people into staying in the fold or join the fold. The reality is, it is just as common if not much more common for things *not* to work out the way we want them to. So when testimonies are wrapped around circumstantial results rather than internal transformations toward Love, then I can't help but be wary. And the narrative that to know God equates to knowing you are a piece of shit has got to die.

A New View
This book (and my life) is my testimony. I discovered the meaning of God when nothing was going "my way." And I grew up believing I was a piece of shit so I didn't need people to convince me that God is part of that equation.

A person's "testimony" is part and parcel with their "baptism"—a transformation into their fullness of being and awareness of unity with our One Human Family. Once you are bold enough to speak to this shift in your life, then you have something worth sharing!

Confession #5: Evangelism: Now Hear This!

Commonly Believed Purpose
Quite literally, this word means "to share the gospel." And gospel means "the good news."

Reality Check
It was not good news to the Native Americans when the European settlers obliterated their land, culture, and way of life—often in the name of God but really in the pursuit of power and profit. Nor was it good news when Africans were enslaved but also forced to worship the same God of their captors. All of this seems obvious to us now. After all, hindsight is 20/20.

But what of today? How are the evangelistic practices of today working or not working?

Firstly, to answer that question you have to define what the "good news" is. And there is a sharp divide in that answer between the far-right evangelicals and progressive, liberal Christians. To the former, the good news essentially means:

Jesus is the only way to salvation. Accept him as your Lord and Savior or fry in hell.

To the latter, the "good news" is more nuanced but goes something like this:

There is life beyond the societal entrapments and personal demons that burden us. Accept God's grace for a new you. Jesus is preferred but not required.

With these definitions in mind, I'm going to give a quick review of three evangelistic methods: witnessing, service work, and mission trips.

Witnessing is not really practiced very much in mainline, left-leaning Christianity. But it is practically a Prime Directive (of the inverse kind from *Star Trek*) for evangelicals. The story I relayed in the previous chapter about witnessing to my Jewish friend in middle school is a great example. Christians with this mindset today typically have a pious view that they *must* convert people to their belief system. They think they are doing the work of God. But if you don't know that you are worshipping an egoic manifestation of God, then you probably don't know that witnessing to others is merely a function of flattering your own Ego.

Both service work and mission trips are done by Christians all along the left/right continuum. These practices involve aiding or supporting people in dire need. Service work is typically done locally and on an ongoing basis. Mission trips take the participants outside of their bubble, usually to an impoverished area regionally or internationally, and are done as a singular event with a hard start and stop.

With the rise of consciousness about the injustice of colonialism in our country's past that was often wrapped in religious pretense, there is a rightful critique of both of these practices. Namely, "doing good" to help others with the ultimate aim of converting them to your religion is disingenuous, manipulative, and sometimes abusive. Yuck. Those are valid concerns supported by centuries of history.

These same concerns are augmented by the fact that many comfortable American Christians today view occasional service work or a mission trip as a box to check off. This is a way of making you feel like you are a deeply caring person and did your part. Polish the halo!

It's easy to go make bricks in sub-Saharan Africa for a week and take lots of selfies with the indigenous people that garner lots of praise (for you) when you post them on Instagram. The impact of that trip wears off about a week after hitting U.S. soil again and you return to your $7 lattes and complaining about the spotty WiFi while you're getting a pedicure. Your feet got really dusty, after all, while you made bricks.

A New View
You may be expecting me to universally pooh-pooh Christian service work and mission trips.

Au contraire!

The service work and mission trips are like the Ford Econoline, remember? They take on the character and intention of the person(s) performing them. There are more than enough suffering people on the planet that the more often good deeds are done, the better. The question is *why* and *how* are these good deeds being performed?

If an individual or organization has the ultimate aim of converting disenfranchised people to their own belief system, I do indeed think that is wrong and woeful. If an individual or organization is using charity as a means to inflate their own sense of importance or value, then that is sad and spiritual "arrested development." If an individual or organization uses these practices for the selfish pursuit of power or profit, it is flat out wicked.

However, if an individual or organization's religious beliefs propel them toward Love and Charity for the least of these,[xv] and such actions are done *without the exploitation or manipulation of those they serve,* then Serve On, brothers and sisters!

I have observed over the years that many of the folks who criticize religious groups for their service work are like armchair quarterbacks. They can tell you what is wrong with what is being done but they themselves are doing nothing. (Pass the Lays potato chips.) If you don't like the way Christians are trying to help others in need, then you better be doing something better yourself.

When our service is informed by Love for all people, our lives become our witness.

And that is all that truly matters.

To paraphrase a quote attributed to St. Francis, *Preach the gospel at all times. When necessary, use words.*

Confession #6: Communion

Commonly Believed Purpose
Communion, The Lord's Supper, or the Eucharist—as it is interchangeably known—is a ritual that Jesus instructed his followers to do in "remembrance" of him.

Reality Check
Full disclosure: Communion is my favorite Christian ritual. I will explain why later. For now, let's look at the lay of the land.

Communion varies wildly in execution and value to different denominations. In the Catholic and Orthodox traditions, it is considered the "sacrament of sacraments." The bread and wine *become* the actual body and blood of Christ in a mystical union during the ritual. Communion is practiced in every Catholic service and in most Orthodox services. There are very strict rules about the production and care of the elements used.

Most American Protestant traditions, on the other hand, view the ritual as merely a symbol of the sacrifice of Jesus' death. Communion is sometimes practiced regularly, such as in the Episcopal tradition, but in most denominations, it is done once a month or quarter, or on special occasions.

The bread can take the form of wafers, matzo crackers, leavened or unleavened loaf bread, or, as is popular amongst Methodists, King's Hawaiian bread. A more recent advent in this tradition is to offer a gluten-free option. (WWJD?) The wine is either con-secrated wine or Welch's grape juice—at least that has been my observation over the years. Welch's, none other!

The distribution of Communion also comes in many forms. In the chapel where I served several years ago, the elements were offered by priests and worship assistants as congregants lined up to receive it. Some churches include a kneeling rail; others do not. Sometimes there is a single cup of wine passed around where people dip their bread, or they may drink directly from the cup. (This latter practice gives me hives.) Baptists love to pass the plates of cracker bits and individual shot glasses of juice through the pews. (That's the heaviest amount of drinking that they will admit to.) I've even seen self-serve communion set up like a buffet table where you can take what you want when you want it.

Trust me, these brief sketches of the variety of communion practices only scratch the surface of the diversity in practice, depth of theological angling, and rules and regulations around the sacrament. I touch on this complexity to illustrate a point. The tradition of communion is, once again, like the Ford Econoline. Clearly, no one group's way of doing it is THE way. So the ritual itself is a vehicle for the meaning that we give it.

When I was coming into the realization that I was an American None, it was during the time I was still serving on the chancel in the aforementioned French Gothic chapel. I slowly was admitting to myself that I didn't believe any of these religious expressions literally. Communion perplexed me the most because I never understood the obsession with the symbolic or literal body and blood of dead Jesus.

Yet, I was transfixed with the ritual.

I truly believed that most people came to the rail with raw honest vulnerability, seeking connection with God. And I considered it a humbling honor to share that intimate moment. As I would serve people, I could see the searching, yearning, surrender, and sometimes angst that only the eyes can expose about one's soul.

Indeed, I felt as though I experienced communion with my fellow human beings, and where there are authentic connections with others, there is Love.

To this day, if I happen to go to a church service for one reason or another, I still deeply value the ritual of communion. But I am a hypocrite. I am not a church member anywhere and do not support, with my time or money, any given institution that may make the practice of communion available to me. I am like someone who rails against paying taxes but enjoys the highways on which they drive, the public education that is offered to their children, and the national parks where they vacation.

A New View

The charge of Jesus to remember him by ingesting his body and blood can be understood in this way: The greatest commandment—to Love, which Jesus embodied—should be as integral to our very being as if it were a molecular part of our DNA. In this way, the body and blood of Jesus become one with ours.

This brings us back to connection. When we Love, we connect. We experience communion.

When this deep understanding becomes one with our consciousness, we *live* communion, regardless of a religious ritual.

Confession #7: Christian Calendar

Commonly Believed Purpose
Wait, say what? There's such a thing as a Christian calendar?

Yes, but it's not sexy firemen holding Bibles.

Reality Check
I would be willing to wager one of my homemade chicken pot pies that the overwhelming number of American Protestant Christians don't realize that there is such a thing as the Christian calendar. The closest thing most Protestants know about is probably Christmas and Easter. Of which, the religious practices and spiritual meanings are in heavy competition with Walmart, Black Friday, and a bevy of fictional characters like Santa, the Elf on the Shelf, and the Easter Bunny.

The lesser-known, originally Christian holidays have also been so commercialized that religious ties have long ago receded. St. Valentine's Day is a boon for the diamond industry and a way for a chick to measure the devotion of her guy. Mardi Gras is topless debauchery set to Dixieland jazz music. St. Patrick's Day is drunk people dressed in green. All Hallow's Eve, aka Halloween, means candy and ready-made costumes for children and an excuse for women to dress up like thematic strippers to the salacious delight of men. Yet to find their stride in American commercialism are even more obscure Christian holy days such as Feast of the Circumcision of Jesus (January 1st) or Feast of the Donkey (January 14th).

The church of my childhood neither taught nor knew, I suspect, of the historical Christian calendar. Imagine my surprise to learn that St. Valentine has a long, albeit oblique, history as an early church martyr, or that Mardi Gras is formally known as Shrove Tuesday and kicks off the repentant season of Lent, or that St. Patrick is responsible for bringing Christianity to Ireland, or that there are *two* back-to-back holy days that honor the dead. All Saints Day (honoring deceased saints) and All Souls Day (honoring the rest of the dead) are teed off by All Hallow's Eve. And this piddly list doesn't include *countless* other days and seasons that are reserved to either honor the life cycle of Jesus (Christmas and Easter being the pinnacle examples) or the memory of Christian figures and special occasions within the church.

In addition to an annual church calendar, the days of the week have symbolism, though this has largely been lost in Western Christianity. Sunday is the anchor day of the week and the only one anyone really knows about. Ancient Christians essentially merged Judaism's Saturday Sabbath with the following day—the day Jesus rose from the dead. Hence, Sunday became a joint day of rest and celebration of Jesus' victory, representing both the end of death and the beginning of new life.

While other days have historical meaning to the church, in reality, a typical, church-going Christian's week looks like this: Go to Church on Sunday and get my Jesus on. Listen intently to the sermon, vow to be a better person this week and carry this shit forward into my life. Monday through Friday, forget everything I heard or committed myself to on Sunday. Get mired in the stress and minutiae of life. Saturday, let it all hang loose because this past week sucked. Party on, Wayne! The following morning at church, *Ok, I'm for real this time.*

A New View
Firstly, the church has failed to keep pace with the evolution of humanity. So if you didn't know about the Christian calendar,

much less its significance, and if you are one of those "Sunday Only Christians," take heart! Short of the age of the martyrs, you are living during the most significant metamorphosis of the religion. There's a lot that's wrong right now and it has nothing to do with you.

With that caveat being said, I find great meaning behind the rituals, traditions, and practices of the Christian calendar. Essentially, both the annual and weekly calendars are a mirror of the life cycle for humans. We are born, we live, we die, ad infinitum. This is both a physical reality but also a spiritual truth. While our bodies will only be born and die once, we have the power of God as Love that regenerates us endlessly during life, if we are spiritually attuned enough to allow it. And even after our death, what we have invested into the world, for better or worse, continues to live on.

Let's just hope that if there's ever a holy day named after you posthumously, that it doesn't get reduced to drunken mayhem, plastic trinkets, and pandemonium at discount stores.

The Dovetail: Parting Thoughts, Summations, and a Send-Off

Over and Out

After 45 years in the business, an icon retired. Heralded as venerable, immutably awesome, and irreplaceable, this historical figure is remembered by a broad swath of the American public— high school athletes, little old ladies from retirement homes, youth groups, surfers, rock bands, carpenters, electricians, florists, travelers, and (clears throat) terrorists.

In 2015, production of the Ford Econoline (which also had been branded the Club Wagon and E-series) ceased. For decades it far outsold any other full-size van due to its reliability and versatility. Whether it transported goods or equipment, groups of people, or (clears throat again) homemade bombs, it truly was irreplaceable. Until, that is, it was replaced.

The new model van was the Ford Transit that boasted far better fuel economy, more horsepower, sophisticated interior electronics, and a sleek body style. The Transit may be a welcome relief as far as interface and utility may go, but I doubt it will ever gain the nostalgia the Econoline earned. The internet is rife with tributes from outdoor adventurers and auto and music industry writers, not to mention what is left unpublished from the minds of ordinary Americans who associate the van with their youth or working adulthood.

This same model van is also mournfully remembered by those who have suffered due to terrorist bombings, DUIs, tragic accidents, and hit and runs. Sadly, there have undoubtedly been reasons to support the *Chester the Molester* appellation. And if you watch any *Law and Order* or *NCIS,* then you know the back of the van is where the dead bodies roll around until they're dumped into a landfill.

Two questions are left in my mind.

What's inside your van? And is it time to upgrade your model?

On Vehicles, the Sacred, and the Ordinary

The point has been driven home (pun intended!) that religious practices are but mere vehicles of the purpose and meaning that we, humans, give them. They are of human origin, inflated to remind us of existential truths, and lastly, aim to return us back to reality with a heightened sense of the sacred. Because I felt increasingly disingenuous at church participating in rituals that seemed conflated and extraneous that were also inextricably interwoven with gratuitous beliefs, I simply had to quit going. But I took the meanings that I gleaned from the rituals with me.

Think of it this way. You are the driver of your van. You decide what that van represents. It begins and ends with you. Eventually, we realize that the van, in the form of fanciful rituals, is not required.

Traditional religious practices are like a good psychotherapist. They should work themselves out of a job. Rituals and traditions ultimately collapse back into mundane reality forcing us to squarely face ourselves. *We* are the van. *We* are the ultimate vehicle for what is right or wrong in the world. Rather than lugging around burdensome, obligatory practices, I challenge us to live our everyday lives as our spiritual practice.

I'll give you an example. I mentioned at the beginning of the chapter that I was essentially an indentured servant (minus the pay or promise to eventually be free) when I was growing up. One of my chores was doing the dishes for our family of five, all day every day it seemed. The weight of oppression and the resentment of being used and taken for granted always felt the heaviest while I stood there, alone, hand washing dish after dish after dish. For many years into my adulthood, I hated doing dishes and would offer to do just about any other chore if someone else would just do the dishes. I could not extract the pain of the past from the task of the present.

Eventually, after my spiritual awakening later in life, I changed the way I viewed washing dishes. As a little treat to myself, I bought a dish soap that had a lavender scent, which I found calming. With every dish I washed, I reflected with gratitude that I had food to eat, children to share a meal with, and running water. I found simple joy in returning a messy plate to its shiny whiteness, like a reminder that I myself am in a constant state of renewal. I scrubbed pots and pans in a circular motion with measured breathing. This stilled my soul and gave me a sense of accomplishment. And I would think about the countless more meals I will share with those I love using these same dishes. Gratitude begat gratitude and pain dissolved.

To this day, *every time* I wash dishes, I practice this ritual of gratitude.

The sacred indwells the ordinary, if we have eyes to see and ears to hear.

Practice Love.

Get Outta My Dreams

I've had many cars over the years. The Little Red Gelcap (Geo Metro) got me through college. My first dream car was a Honda

Civic and my second was a Volkswagen Jetta. During my second divorce, I was homeless with three children living out of a Mercedes GL 550. The irony was not lost on me. After that divorce, I got a car whose color I called F.U. Blue because my ex-husband would never let me have a blue car. Thankfully, I am long past pain associated with my vehicles. You would love my current car. It is a lovely, small SUV that I affectionately call Blanche.

Like the cars that I have left behind, so have I abandoned the pain and suffering that used to define me. And it is to that subject that we now travel.

CHAPTER 5

PAIN

Looks like a happy childhood pic, right? Well before the insulating wall of social media, photographs could still mask bottomless pain. This one photo alone conjures multiple deeply sad memories.

Opener: Addiction to Affliction

For most of my life, I carried around a disfiguring growth on my person. This frightened many people away from me, seemed benign to a few, and was an invitation to exploit me to others.

It was large, ever-expanding, menacingly ugly, and demanded control of my thoughts, feelings, and actions. Because I had grown up with this affliction, it seemed normal, albeit at times uncomfortable. Unbeknownst to me, I did many things that contributed to its constant growth. It affected my breathing and ability to eat. It also affected my vision. I would see the world and others through this obstruction, often leading me to veer off a well-intentioned course and plummet right into self-destruction.

This aberration nearly killed me before it was eventually excised.

I wonder if you suffer from this same debilitating affliction. It has a name.

Pain.

Menu and Music: The Meat of the Matter

Pain is the meat of the matter. Seriously, if it weren't for pain, humans would have little motivation to seek out spirituality or God. So it is fitting that the main course on our menu is a meaty attribution to the chapter on pain.

Very few things say "Welcome Home" better than a Southern slow-cooked pot roast. Imagine the stress of the rat race in the big city and then finally making it out to Grandma's house in the country. This is where you can just exhale and enjoy some home-cooked goodness.

Here's what Grandma probably hasn't ever explained to you. When you start with a big ol' hunkin' slab of chuck roast, in all its raw and marbly glory, the initial sting of searing the flesh to lock in the juices just launches the path to succulent greatness. What follows is a long cooking process where the meat slowly contracts under immense environmental tension, and if you take it off the flame too early, you will think it is tough and over-cooked. The trick is you have to cook the roast past this phase and the roast will relax, creating a tender, melt in your mouth, gastro-sensation.

Pain functions in a similar way, particularly accumulated life pain. There is a process—an arc if you will—whereby you recognize, accept, and release the pain that lends itself to happy freedom.

Did I just compare your worst life experience to a pot roast? Yes, I'm afraid I did.

Crank some "Joy and Pain" and follow along to the beat and hope of Rob Bass while your Obsequious Pot Roast is cooking.

The Backstory: Pain Before Gain

Firstly, let me say—this is the hardest chapter for me to write. No, it's not because it is painful for me to talk about pain. In fact, I may be one of the happiest people ever to write about pain. But that is only because I used to be deep-fried, LDL-saturated in Pain and have made it to the other side.

The challenge in writing this chapter is that I have so much I want to say about the subject of Pain. Therefore, the scope of this chapter will be limited to a high-level treatment of Pain's relationship with Christianity and how I now understand the bane of human existence.

Let's start by defining our terms.

Pain, with a lowercase p, is an initial reaction to a stimulus that causes one mental, emotional, physical, or spiritual harm or extreme discomfort. This could be the kind of pain one feels when you pick up a hot pan without a pot holder, or the sharp sting of rejection after someone breaks up with you, or the immeasurable grief you feel upon the death of a loved one. It can come in more subtle forms, leaving an imprint in your psyche, like when your romantic partner says something passive aggressive or a maître d' tacitly makes a racist excuse that there is no more seating available.

It is entirely normal—and human—to feel pain in these ways. How you manage normal pain though, determines the power, growth, and gravity of the other type of Pain.

Pain, with a capital P, is a symbiotic agency within your being that you carry forward from accumulated or inherited small-p pain. It grows within you and continually seeks validation. The reason I say it is symbiotic with you is that we feed it knowingly or unknowingly. We feed Pain with our unhealthy thoughts, indulgent emotions, and flaccid spirit. These fuel sources ultimately derive from Fear.

We accumulate scores of small-p pain experiences during our lifetime and if this is not correctly counterbalanced with the power of Love along the way, the small p's amass to create one ginormous, evil MF'r. Think of the villain Imhotep in The Mummy, who garners his menacing presence with infinite grains of sand. Individually, a grain of sand causes no harm. But harnessed as a collective power, it destroys everything in its wake.

Big-P Pain is quite literally a life sucking leech.

Pain was like my invisible conjoined twin growing up. Because I couldn't see it as a child, I thought it was a normal part of me, not knowing that Pain definitely had a mind and will of its own. It started much smaller than me but quickly grew to mirror my own size, causing me endless conflict as it whispered sinister things in my ear. By adulthood, Pain dwarfed me in size, trying to strangle me with its oppressive, suffocating weight.

As a kid, Pain chronically manifested in the forms of wincing stomach aches and crippling headaches. Walking home from elementary school felt like walking death row. Doom awaited me. I never knew if, when I got home, my stepdad would have received a word from God and had divine justification to beat me.

After being homeschooled and isolated for two years in early high school, I had constant suicidal ideations. I was physically incapable of smiling, except when I was in the presence of my stepdad and mom. A forced smile was required at that time. I wanted to die but I didn't want to be berated or beaten. Death seemed preferable.

By the time I was on my own in college, Pain had begun getting too big for its britches and was a sassy pants, being bossy and all. Pain would overcome me as if it owned me, even when I had no present threatening circumstances. Sudden fits of emotional implosion would befall me and I would vanish into a deep, dark vortex of contorted thinking and feeling. When I was in that space, it seemed there was no way out.

Many times, I found myself crying inconsolably while staring into a mirror with complete self-loathing, hating my very existence. I would claw and pull at my face, wanting to remove it.

I dreaded going to bed because of the horror-film quality of nightmares that were sure to engulf me in my sleep. I would wake up in pools of sweat, terrified of the alternate universe that I had experienced. The theme of the dreams was nearly always the same. Someone (often stepdad or a proxy) was violently trying to kill me while I was attempting to save my three younger brothers and escape. Meanwhile, my mom stood in a dark corner and silently watched it all.

Like an unwitting Starship Enterprise officer, I had become a host to an invasive alien being who, at its capricious will, would overtake my thoughts, feelings, and (sometimes) actions. To the outside world, I functioned as an ambitious, energetic young adult but beneath the dynamic exterior, I was an open, pulsating, bloody, raw-tissue wound. In retrospect, I believe I was enduring Post-Traumatic Stress Disorder (PTSD) from my abusive childhood.

A measure of relief came in my early-mid 20s when I was diagnosed and medically treated for a form of depression. This coupled with counseling helped me significantly. After a few years of treatment, I weaned off of medication and therapy because I no longer fought bouts of upended emotions. I felt like I had found an equilibrium and a new lease on life.

But Pain is cunning, my friends. My Pain was like the Borg meets Homey the Clown. It adapts to survive and it knew that I, Rachel, "don't play that" anymore. The manifestations of self-loathing and erratic emotional sinkholes had been dealt with (or so I thought). I wouldn't succumb to those specific behaviors anymore so my Pain took the form of the religious good girl who was going to pray and behave perfectly.

This Homey the Borg iteration of Pain reached its zenith in Marriage #2. I clung to pious ideals, an inflated view of my own virtue, and religious rules for dear life, much like Sandra Bullock clinging to the exterior of her space station in Gravity after ricocheting frenetically in the dark void. I thought if I exemplified a "good" Christian and followed all the church's directions, my life would be great. I'd have a faithful, kind husband; obedient, joyful children; and I, myself, would be perfectly trim, with perfectly coiffed hair, and have perfectly prepared home-cooked meals every night of the week for my adoring family—or some hogwash like that.

There's a holy host that is wrong with that construct. For starters, it is transactional and unrealistic but I will save that dissection for another time. What I want to focus on now is how what appears to be noble on the outside (desire for a happy family and being a "good" girl) was actually a devious presentation of Pain making me its bitch.

Basically, Pain had learned that if it couldn't kill me by taking me to obviously dark places, it would fool me into believing I was in the light while rotting me from within. As much as it pains me to say this, the Church and modern, evangelical Christianity was a prime medium for this nasty ruse.

Every time Husband #2 threatened to leave me homeless and penniless and take the children away from me, the Church taught me to pray for him and shower him with love privately. By "love," they meant meek submission. Every time he demeaned me verbally and debased me sexually, claiming that it was my role to please him however he saw fit, I was to acquiesce quietly. The many times that I was afraid he would try to kill me, I was supposed to be grateful that at least it had been a while since the previous incident. His methodical destruction of all my relationships with friends and family meant that he just needed me to love him more. His manipulative refusals for me to have interests or activities outside the home fortified that my role was within the house.

According to Megachurchland and this form of Christian teaching, I was an exemplary Christian wife. The resentment that was building, the decay of my sense of self, and the encroaching darkness in my soul were viewed as evidence that I was not trusting in the Lord enough nor rejoicing in all things.

Hell no, I wasn't rejoicing in all things. And I was trusting in the wrong God.

You see, Pain is a minion for Ego which is an agent of Fear. I had attached my identity to the notion of being a saint-beyond-reproach while subjecting myself to torrents of daily abuse for years. I had taken pride in being "good" and not behaving like my husband. My sense of purpose was attached to my conjoined twin Pain because it fed my Ego that I was valuable by being a martyr. That is some subversive shit.

The time came to lock and load and make Pain my bitch.

Confessions

Confession #1: Joel Osteen and Mother Teresa

"God wants us to prosper financially, to have plenty of money, to fulfill the destiny He has laid out for us." —Joel Osteen

"Pain and suffering have come into your life, but remember pain, sorrow, and suffering are but the kiss of Jesus—a sign that you have come so close to Him that He can kiss you." —Mother Teresa

Both Joel and Mother Teresa got what they believed God wanted for them. Joel's four-member family lives in a 17,000-square-foot mansion on a large gated lot, he drives a Ferrari amongst other cars, jet sets in his private plane, and has teeth sparklier than a 1980s game show host.

Mother Teresa spent a lifetime living amongst the world's most indigent people in the densely populated, squalid slums of

Calcutta, India and relished her poverty. Both have claimed to be full-time servants of the same God.

Osteen claims that God's greatest desire for people is to rise above, reaching every level of success possible. Mother Teresa has an almost opposite perspective elevating personal suffering as the tantamount expression of intimacy with Jesus (who is God to her).

This dichotomy of "opulence versus destitution" as the prime fulfillment of Christianity can also be quantified as "pain avoidant versus pain seeker." These polarizing manifestations of Christianity became strikingly evident to me when I left Megachurchland (akin to Osteen) and returned to my progressive seminary (akin to Mother Teresa). Theologically speaking, this is the "prosperity gospel" versus "social justice gospel."

I never bought into the prosperity gospel, the notion that if you believe enough, pray enough, and send your money to XYZ televangelist, then God will return it to you tenfold. That was always slimy to me. But it was equally absurd to me that I had to volunteer for a life of hardship to have a close relationship with God.

I will never forget an exchange I had with one of my professors while I was finishing my master's degree. This professor had done impressive work initiating a movement within mainline Christianity that inspired seminarians to live, work, and socialize amongst marginalized people. This enables them to serve those most in need, which is what the social justice gospel is all about. I had lamented to my professor about the hardships of single motherhood and the dangerous scenarios that I faced with my ex-husband. As much as I admired her work, I was not prepared for her response to my personal concerns.

She suggested that I move my three children into a "new monastic" community in one of Dallas' most impoverished, crime-ridden neighborhoods. She said that I could live amongst other seminarians serving the local residents and that I would have a built-in support network. I left that meeting incredulous at what an astoundingly dumb idea that was. It was like telling a starving person to flog themselves for good measure.

I do not believe in linking relationship with God to the pursuit or acquisition of wealth. Nor do I believe volunteering for a depressed, downtrodden life is necessary. (Life is hard enough, thank you.) Instead, I believe in aligning myself with Love, which includes compassionately serving those in need. This can be achieved while maintaining a balance that allows for the open-ended, fun exploration of all the abundant possibilities life offers. Life is not a zero-sum game.

While some people may be genuinely motivated and fulfilled to dedicate the whole of their lives to social justice issues, I would rather see more people doing some work toward social justice, while maintaining personal balance in their lives, than fewer people doing most of the work. The latter paradigm sets up unrealistic expectations of those who serve. This causes burnout for the few who are serving and renders the idea of serving undesirable for those who are not.

Pain should neither be something to avoid nor are we obliged to seek it. The more important question is, how do we manage it when it inevitably happens? And if managed properly, we will become more compassionate toward others who suffer.

Confession #2: This is Not a Test

You are not being "tested" by God.

Christians love to debate whether or not hardship is caused or allowed by God, as if it's a test of your "Christianness."

This way of thinking presupposes the egoic, external-otherness notion of God—the kind of God who is a deity that has desires, has a plan for your life, and brokers deals. What's really going on when people say that God is testing them is usually one of two things.

Primarily, they are trying to make sense of why something "bad" has happened. So it's easy to say God is testing you, although that rings of false humility. (Some Christians say that if you are being tested by God, then you are favored by him.) Secondly, this is a gross misdirection. We are conveniently taking the attention away from any personal or large-scale humankind culpability that may have engendered the given situation.

Understanding "trials and tribulations" (common Christian parlance) as tests from God originates from various scriptures. This would be another instance in which the Bible is either being misconstrued or is merely wrong, reflecting an ancient way of conceiving God.

Thinking that God was testing me during my abusive marriage deflected my own responsibility about my own dysfunctions that led me to marry such a man. If a person gets cancer, it is tragic biology, not God toying with a person's fortitude. If a married man is tempted to sleep with his secretary, it may be a test of his character and values but it is not a test from God.

The acceptance of pain and hardship as a natural part of living was liberating to me. It freed me from an outdated, ill-functioning notion of God and empowered me toward healing. I can't control other people or most situations. But I can control myself and how I respond to pain.

Small-p pain just is. We choose how it functions.

Confession #3: The Suffering of Jesus Wasn't What You Think

The Christian season of Lent, which precedes Easter, is essentially an homage to the suffering of Jesus during his capture, torture, and execution by the Romans. This is classically referred to as "The Passion of Christ." The word "passion" originally meant "suffering" before it took on the form of "intense emotion" that we use today.

In Catholic churches, agonizing portrayals of his crucifixion provide morbid reminders of his experience. And while Baptist and other evangelical denominations say they prefer to focus on Jesus' triumphant resurrection, a plethora of their hymns and sermons nonetheless extol the graphic nature of bloody flogging, nails through the hands and feet, a crown of thorns, and asphyxiation. (If you've ever driven through the Deep South, you are bound to see a billboard with some close-up graphic of a bloody hand nailed to a wooden beam and a proclamation that Jesus died for you.)

This fixation on blood and gore as it relates to Jesus is not wholly a misnomer. Most religions deal with anguish and pain in some way or other. After all, religion aims to help us make sense of our experience on Earth.

The issue I have with the treatment of Jesus's suffering is how it is commonly interpreted—Jesus underwent excruciating physical pain, all for you, to the point of death. The suffering he endured was a saintly sacrifice on his part for you and your lousy sins.

There are nuances to this belief, of course. Some churches believe that Jesus couldn't have actually felt physical pain because he was God, after all. Some recognize the human side of Jesus and almost boast that of course he felt immeasurable physical pain, that's how dang awesome he was, that he went through all of that for you, you piece of pond scum. Some churches go so far to say that not only did Jesus feel pain, but he felt the most exaggerated pain a human could ever feel because he incurred the weight of all the sin in the world, past, present or future, when he was crucified.

Or... there's this interpretation...

Jesus was a human who underwent extreme physical pain as would any human who experienced the same treatment. But his greatest pain was not physical torture and his greatest regret for premature death was not fear of dying. When he is said to have cried out, "Father, Father, why have you forsaken me?," it was not because he thought God had him killed.

Rather, imagine Jesus dying on the cross, surrounded by both the Romans and the local Jewish people who had turned on him. As he surveyed these people, his all-consuming, piercing pain was heartache. He had walked and preached a message of Love and inclusivity. What gut-wrenching, soul-splitting, endless agony to know this Love but to see the masses reject its truth and power. In modern times, Gandhi and Martin Luther King, Jr. faced a similar dynamic. Personally, this became illuminating to me when I knew this Love but had to helplessly watch someone I loved self-destruct due to addictions, ignorance, and Fear.

And when Jesus cried out to God, I imagine his greatest lament was that Jesus knew his work was not done. He wanted to teach people Love, show people Love, and he did not get to see his work come to fruition. There was so much more Love to share. Jesus knew that this mission was his life calling so it must have grieved and confounded him beyond words that his life was cut short.

The Passion of Christ was indeed intense emotion—even suffering if you will—but it was far less about his physical pain and much more about the Love he knew that he wished everyone else knew too.

Confession #4: Guess My Greatest Pain

As a child, I was routinely beaten. I was sexually abused, shamed, and marginalized. I was frequently ridiculed, derided, and discounted. As a teen, I knew what it was like to chronically go without lunch at school and to eat popcorn for dinner because there was nothing else. As a young adult, I fought depression, being underemployed, having a stalker, and generally being dazed and confused.

My 30s ushered in a series of misfortunes including a Peeping Tom (a dude from Megachurchland no less), divorce #1, an abusive marriage, divorce #2, the loss of (supposed) friends and church affiliation, and traumatized children to care for. The beginning of my 40s had me harboring the weight of the world trying to survive financially alone with three children, constantly fielding off the torment of my ex-husband, reinventing myself in the workplace out of nothing, and surviving sexual assault from an employer. And those are just the obvious obstacles.

Out of all that, which event do you suppose caused me the greatest pain?

Physical abuse? Sexual abuse? Emotional or mental abuse? Economic abuse?

Ok, it's not fair of me to ask you that because it's a trick question.

Several years ago, I would have told you that none of that was my greatest pain—by a long shot. I would have said that the subversion of Christianity handily took that designation. When the very thing that is supposed to "save" you destroys you, you are left not knowing who or what to trust, as if the fabric of the universe turned out to be a farce. I would have said that spiritual abuse was exceedingly the most profound harm I have endured in my life.

Today I award spiritual abuse second place next to the grand prize winner. My greatest pain was the death of Pain.

The delineation of The Plano Experience illustrates how I grabbed Pain by the balls and ripped it out of my being. Leading up to that pivotal event were months of Pain's attempt to outlast my increasing resolve to eradicate it by manifesting itself in physical, mental, and emotional anguish. It was the most harrowing hardship I have ever endured because Pain had been rooted, like fibrous connective tissue, in my body, mind, and spirit for the entire duration of my life. It was like trying to uproot a 500-year-old oak tree and still leave the ground intact. And yeah, that's gotta hurt.

The Plano Experience

This is the story of how I made Pain my bitch.

It had been several months since I left Husband #2. After surviving a virtual diaspora, the children and I were finally settled into a rental home. My two youngest were preschool age and I did everything I could to maintain a sense of normalcy for them: play dates, crafts, story times, cooking together, and so on.

But on the inside, I was The Walking Dead. (Cue the zombie sounds.) I was in a catatonic state, absorbing glaring truths that I had previously denied. My fantasy marriage and life were precisely that—never real according to the ideals to which I had held them. Megachurchland was an uncaring, pompous sham. I had no family, no support system nearby. I was now responsible for raising and supporting three children after nearly a decade of being a stay-at-home mom. I had no idea how I would survive, much less sustain a life for my children that was comfortable and relatively carefree.

I had exchanged one hell for another.

When I garnered what little shrapnel of strength I had to leave Husband #2, not only was I standing up to him but I was also standing up to a lifetime of dysfunction, abuse, and wait for it... wait for it... Say hello to my little friend... Pain.

Pain didn't like me daring to oppose it. The measure it took to pick myself up and leave was matched by Pain's violent roar and aggression. Pain wanted to play rough.

And play rough it did.

What used to be an invisible conjoined twin that sinisterly whispered in my ear had now been absorbed into my body. Having Pain fully indwell my person was physically painful. My body ached, throbbing with raw nerves on a 24/7 basis. I carried a relentless heaviness that was palpable, like living on a planet with 50 times the gravity of Earth. I hadn't been able to eat or sleep for many months. My throat was constricted as if every breath or swallow was an impossible task. By all accounts, I was indeed the living dead.

Pain was no longer an abstraction that malevolently toyed with me. I was now its biological host. If it couldn't control me, it wanted to be me.

The last time I had felt this despondent was during my home-schooled incarceration as a teen. Only this time the stakes were higher. History was repeating itself— yet again, I was responsible for three other young lives. And this time, they weren't my brothers but my children.

Suicide was not an option, yet I resented having to live. I had been to counseling on and off my entire adulthood and had been on antidepressants during my second marriage. Nevertheless, I found myself worse off than I'd ever been.

I had determined that the present problem was something that counseling or prescription drugs could not fix. Therefore, I chose to go through my darkest season, as an adult, with neither.

One night while my children slept upstairs, I was tossing and turning as usual around 2:00 a.m. unable to find rest. I saw no end in sight of my debilitating affliction. I had become a shell of a person and was 100% faking my way as a mother and a human being. For both my own health and my children, I could no longer live this way.

So in the wee hours of a chilly autumn night in the cookie-cutter suburb of Plano, Texas, I waged a war of cosmic proportions.

I was fed up and had nothing to lose. I threw the covers off and began pacing the floor. I had a few words to say to Pain—out loud with every microfiber of intention and power in my being.

I will NOT give my life to YOU.

You will not control me! Leave me, leave my body, leave my thoughts, leave my heart. NOW.

My power is NOT of YOU. My Power is of LOVE.

BE GONE.

You evil force of darkness, LEAVE ME NOW AND FOREVER.

I walked back and forth, my voice rising, gesturing my hands with emphatic conviction. I was DONE with this motherfucker.

LOVE consume me, I invoked. *Pain LEAVE ME*, I commanded.

I do NOT belong to you.

I repeated these commands with greater conviction and resolve. I think my tirade lasted no more than a few minutes. I paused, panting, and stood still. My arms by my side with palms open. I had just mustered up the velocity of a spiritual tornado in my bedroom.

And then it happened.

Starting at the crown of my head, a tingling sensation began to wash down my body. It was a thing. It felt like a palpable energy or force that descended down and through me. And like a swoosh, it expelled from the soles of my feet, diffusing into the nocturnal ethers.

I kid you not, the body aches? GONE.

The heaviness? Gone.

The constriction in my throat? Gone.

I was light. I was FREE.

I quite literally felt 50 pounds lighter.

I stood there for a moment, waiting to see if it would come back. It didn't. I stood there a moment longer. I was in shock and disbelief.

So, guess what I did?

I went to the kitchen and ate a bag of Natural Cheetos. It was the most I had eaten in one sitting in nearly a year. I ate my Cheetos and laughed. I couldn't believe it. That evil energy was gone. There is a power of Love and Life that is greater than anything that challenges it. Holy crap.

And then I went to sleep. Sweet sleep.

You may be scratching your head about now. You are probably thinking, but I thought she was rational and no-nonsense and doesn't believe in hocus pocus. Well, I'd like to think that I am both of those things. But what I discovered in this experience was that we have access to unlimited power to overcome darkness if we tap into it and yield to it.

I had stepped out in faith to access this power—the power of Love—and told Pain to go stick it where the sun don't shine. I don't exactly know how or what happened but I am absolutely certain of one thing. The living-death grip that had eviscerated my soul and tried to convince me that death was preferable to life will NEVER own me again!

Confession #5: I Am My Own Worst Enemy

One of the salient features of the maturation process is when you realize that you and you alone are responsible for who you are and what you are doing with your life. When we quit casting outwards and turn inwards, embracing self-accountability, we unleash counter-intuitive freedom. This liberation, when fueled by Love, propels us to new levels of being and living. This is where the magic happens.

Before evolving to that place, we must understand who our real enemy is. Big P Pain tries relentlessly to convince us that other people and external circumstances are to blame for our miseries. Putting aside the rare situation where a person is truly a victim of another person or event, the overarching, broad truth is that most of our troubles originate in that space between our ears, which happens to be home base for Pain.

Earlier, I used the imagery of Pain as an invisible conjoined twin that whispers in your ear. Technically, Pain originates from your egoic mind that, of course, is biologically associated with your brain. Regardless of how you want to conceive this, Pain is the voice in your head that isn't doing you any favors. And this Pain is an extension of you, not the doings of other people or circumstances. They're too busy with their own Pain in the brain anyway.

Confession #6: Pain is Like a Bad Perm

You gotta outgrow it.

In the '80s there was a hair identity crisis. Amongst other filament foibles of the time, the crowned jewel was the godforsaken PERM. Everybody from John Oates to Barbra Streisand to Bon Jovi (and many more) were sporting them.

As was I during the Econoline period. There are some things one should never do at home. Getting a perm is one of those things.

I suppose to save money, my mother had the pastor's wife, who was known for her perming prowess, come over to crown me with a blessed bulb of curls. This harrowing process took hours.

First, she methodically rolled slivers of my long, thick hair onto bright pink curlers. Then the chemical processing phase began. After squirting god-knows-what on my head, I was left in a cloud of fumes. My eyes watered and burned. I could barely breathe.

And while the curls were incubating, the chemicals were slowly eating away at the flesh around the hairline on my forehead.

"It will all be worth it," I kept telling myself.

Finally, when the time came to release the curlers—be free ye agents of hair bondage!— I imagined my beautiful hair would cascade down my body in lovely, loose curly locks (think Brooke Shields or Meg Ryan in the '80s). But no, my hair turned out more like Richard Simmons.

So I was left with bloodshot eyes, chemical burns on my forehead, lung damage, and looking like a Chia Pet.

I learned never to attempt mixing chemicals and hair at home. There are professionals for that. And even at the tender age of 14, I learned that a bad hairstyle does not define me. Hair keeps growing, thankfully. (No offense to Richard Simmons who has owned that 'do like a boss for decades.) The bad perm experience also initiated the slow-to-learn life lesson not to take myself too seriously.

Natural, normal pain should function much in the same way as my bad perm. We experience something injurious (the perm process), deal with its ramifications (living with that perm), learn from it (my bad perm did not become my identity), and then let go of it (new unpermed hair springeth forth).

However, Pain would be the equivalent of me continuing to perm my hair over and over again to the point where my hair is fried and it falls out, all the while deluding myself about how beautiful I look. The decision to remove Pain from your life by changing your mental and behavioral habits doesn't mean that the recovery process is easy but the end results are exceedingly worth it.

Confession #7: The Plague of the West

Have you ever experienced being lonely in a relationship? To the point where you determine you'd rather be lonely alone than lonely with someone? If so, you are not alone. Numerous headlines about the epidemic of loneliness in our country populate news feeds regularly these days. We are feeling this cosmic punch in the gut together—yet alone—it seems.

There is a relationship between this phenomenon and my journey to become a None. Abandoning Christianity was a long, drawn-out process because I liked the "idea" of belonging to a spiritual community. Despondency set in as I grew fatigued from feeling like an outsider while being on the inside. I decided I'd rather be wandering in the spiritual wilderness alone than live with the stress and disconnect of being lonely within my own religion.

Returning to Saint Teresa of Calcutta, she rocked the western world with the observation that "the greatest suffering is being lonely, feeling unloved, having no one." She considered this to be the Western world's extreme form of poverty, harder to cure than disease, homelessness, or hunger. There are tangible solutions to the latter problem but the plague of the West is solved only with Love, which requires a transformation of the human spirit.

How much more profound this observation is when the Church itself has created an inhospitable environment for the vast amount of 21st-century Americans, alienating scores of people due to its obsolescent beliefs and practices, self-serving interests, and cultural irrelevance.

The Dovetail: Parting Thoughts, Summations and a Send Off

Mad Cow Disease

Psst. Psst.

Can I talk to you for a minute? Over here in private?

Thanks. Pardon my hushed tone but there's something really awkward going on here. There's an elephant in the room.

Ok, well not in the room. In the chapter. And it's not an elephant. It's a cow. And, I don't know about you, but she's been silently judging me from the corner over there this whole time. She's sitting on a stool, with her hind legs crossed, staring me up and down batting those long, bovine lashes with contempt as if saying, "Oh no you di'nt." I swear, she even gave me a triple Z snap.

Have you noticed too? Surely it's not just me.

Phew. Ok, we can talk freely now. It's funny how when you acknowledge something uncomfortable its power diminishes. I used the analogy in the opening of this chapter on pain as being the meat of the matter, explaining why I assigned a meat dish to this topic. That little play on words may be slightly amusing at best but the bigger irony of the meat dish is not lost on me.

A cow literally died so that you and I could enjoy eating it. Not only that, depending on the source of that cow, it may have had subpar living conditions and suffered inhumane treatment before making its way to our plates.

Don't worry, I'm not about to get all judgy and political on you. After all, I'm the one who put beef on the menu! I do my best to live in reality and the reality is that 95% of Americans eat meat.

Americans may love meat but we fear pain. Our wildly consumerist society has yielded all-time high records of opioid addictions and suicides in our attempt to eschew discomfort or pain and find fulfillment. (Maybe a cheeseburger will make me feel better?)

Our relationship with meat hints toward America's relationship with pain. In short, there is a disconnect and short-term satisfaction may lead to long-term demise.

Eighty percent of Americans live in urban areas. I may be taking liberty here, but I think it is fair to say that most of the 80% have never seen live chickens, cows, and pigs, much less been to a farm or a production facility. Flawlessly processed meat just appears in their local grocery store free from feathers, hides, and "parts." This bypass creates a hollow appreciation of meat both in terms of the complex production system that made it affordable and available but also in terms of the sentient animal who died for their meal.

If we were to know the origins of our meat, appreciating the associated pain or loss of life of the animal, then our experience eating it would likely be more fulfilling. Sitting down to a home-cooked meal summons a greater depth of gratitude for the life force being ingested and repurposed in the form of your pot roast. Similarly, when we know pain and choose to face it, not fear it, we can allow pain to convert as energy for nourishing the growth of our being. As far as I see it, both eating meat and pain are a natural part of human living.

With the advent of an industrialized society in the late 19th century, Americans began hoovering meat and animal byproducts (dairy and eggs) like they were going out of style. This new anchor of the American diet contributed to increased life expectancies and billions of delighted taste buds. Meat is now commonplace in every meal of the day for many Americans.

Americans comprise one-fifteenth of the world's population but devour a third of the world's meat. This excessive consumption has been proven to be intricately linked to heart disease, cancer, and obesity. Diet fads aside, many nutritionists now advise the moderate intake of meat and animal products as part of healthy, balanced eating. Interestingly, meat "helped make us what we are, but now it can help unmake us."

Moderate meat in your diet is like small p pain. It is a natural part of life and can help grow and strengthen you. Excessive meat intake is like Big P Pain. It accumulates over time from singular incidents and then takes on the form of something larger than the sum of its parts yielding harm to your health or life.

My family and I are committed reducetarians. We overwhelmingly eat a plant-based diet but occasionally incorporate responsibly raised meat or animal products into our meals. Different members of our family had different reasons of supreme importance for making this choice—it lessens the environmental impact due to livestock production, it is a statement against the inhumane treatment of animals, and eating less meat improves personal health. So on the special occasion that we enjoy a slow-cooked pot roast, for example, we share such a meal with heightened intentionality.

May we humbly and responsibly appreciate both the gift of meat in our diets and the gift of pain as an impetus for growth.

On Gnats and Taming the Beast

Have you ever walked down a sidewalk in Texas in the middle of a hot July day? You'll notice a couple of distinct things. First, sweat oozes from your pores due to the oppressive humidity. Second, there are those dagnabit gnats. Oh, you'll see them whizzing around in an indistinct cloud before you pass through them. Except you don't pass through them because they follow you, similar to Pigpen's dust cloud. And unless you can hold your breath until you reach your indoor destination, you will inevitably inhale some. After years of living in the South, I have come to accept it's unavoidable.

Small p pain, too, is unavoidable in life. I have found that expecting there will be occasional gnat clouds and knowing that I'll have to swallow a few to get through them has lessened their impact on my path in life. It just comes with the territory and more ardently fuels me on my journey.

I shared with you in The Plano Experience how I expunged Big P Pain from my being. But I need to be forthright about something. It is said that you never lose your demons, you just learn how to live with them. (Thanks Dr. Strange, bald Tilda Swinton, and the world of Marvel.) Big P Pain no longer dwells within me and nor is it my commensurate conjoined twin. Instead, it is like a shriveled appendage, mostly devoid of energy. But occasionally, with the right amalgam of triggers, it rummages up enough momentum of its own and tries to mess with me.

When this happens, I return to the comfort of knowing that I, fueled by Love, can rise above and once more, tell that sniveling, conniving, Poor Excuse of Gray Matter Energy to GTFO. And then I go about my business of being a grateful, happy, happy person, gnats and all!

You Are Not the Boss of Me

Pain is not the boss of me. I have made that clear. I hope you reach the same conviction too. Love is my boss, fallible though I may be.

A funny thing happens when Love is your boss. Life is brighter, lighter, and well, FUN. As Mavis Staples says, "No more sorrow, no more Pain! Always joy, joy, joy!"

I love living and part of what makes it so fun is exploring the many facets of what it is to be human. What could be more titillating or exciting than cannonballing right into the subject of Vices and Vanities? Don't be skeered. We all have some.

CHAPTER 6

VICES AND VANITIES

As soon as I was out of my childhood home, I have worn a costume for Halloween every single year. Sometimes other people (uh-hmm, sorry guys!) were dragged along with my exuberance.

Opener: Augmented Aspirations

In college, I was a founding member of a distinguished organization. You could say it was somewhat philosophical in nature uniting people of similar attributes. We didn't do much other than just celebrate what made us unique.

To gain membership, you had to be endowed with a few qualifying certitudes. Value is measured by quality, not quantity. Diminutive details create aggregate beauty. The peaks in life sometimes aren't as big as we want but we appreciate what has been bequeathed to us nonetheless. Small and mighty is not to be underestimated. These flat pronouncements roused our group with a robust purpose.

Not a single man met our standards nor did most women. Chances are you wouldn't either. In fact, we only had three members.

The name of our esteemed collective?

The Itty Bitty Titty Committee.

Though we were small in many ways, life had massive revelations yet to come.

Menu and Music: Liquid Spirit

Choosing a cocktail recipe for the chapter on vices was as obvi as Sylvester Stallone playing a tough guy in a movie. I mean, if we're going to get down and dirty, this is the place to do it. Turns out though, there's an even greater reason for this pairing beyond alcohol's sordid reputation with vice.

Let's look at the etymologies of three keywords. *Liquor* and its related form *liquid* derived from the Latin verb *liquere,* which means "to be fluid." The term *spirit,* commonly pluralized in relation to alcohol, traces back to Middle Eastern alchemists of antiquity. They were not trying to convert lead into gold; rather, they were in pursuit of medicinal elixirs. The vapors from the distillation process were considered the "spirit" of the base alcoholic liquid. *Alcohol* has parallel origins from both French and Arabic, meaning "a distilled or rectified spirit."

How fitting it is that the term "spirit" plays a dual role in our discussion at hand. I'm no alchemist but it is my utmost conviction that spiritual vitality is the elixir for a joyful, content life. A fluid, non-binary approach to the exploration of vices and vanities is requisite for a balanced view on the subject. And just like the distillation process of liquor, our relationship with vices and vanities extract and reveal our true essence.

Americans are notorious for the EOD drink after a long day at work. Whether it's Happy Hour with friends and colleagues or a glass of wine at home, this is one of the ways that we "unwind" and "relax." After all, all work and no play make Jack a dull boy.

But the "work hard, play hard" ethos has come at a price for our culture and individual lives in many ways. In a digital age where we are tethered to our devices and by extension, anchored to our work, we are in greater need than ever for balance and congruency in the way that we live.

When we become extreme in one area of our lives it affects, usually for the worse, other areas. Therefore, I seek to offer a non-judgmental look at some of the classic expressions of vices and vanities through a realistic lens about their merits and detractions.

The Balancing Act aperitif sets the tone for our discussion at hand. There is also a mocktail version if that's your preference.

One of my favorite internet memes is, "Alcohol: Because no great story started with someone eating a salad." Life is colorful and we make it much more so with our vices and vanities. So, raise your glasses because in the spirit of Alan Jackson, *It's Five O'clock Somewhere!* Cheers to Life! Cheers to YOU!

The Backstory: A Tale of Two Titties

I bet you didn't anticipate that my boobs would feature so prominently in my tell-all treatise about spirituality and religion. And yet, here we are.

The undulating adventure with my boobies began around the age of 14 when both the outlook of my chest and spirits were equally deflated. This was when I was being homeschooled. Like I said earlier, it was an exceptionally bleak time. Perhaps the only silver lining, from my teenage perspective, was that at least I wasn't at school where I felt so self-conscious about my flat chest. And when I say I was flat chested, I was an A-*minus* cup!

I reasoned to myself that I was just a late bloomer so I fervently did my bust exercises to expedite things. For those of you not in the know, you cup your hands together while squeezing a tennis ball and bend your elbows at a 90-degree angle while pumping them toward one another. The greater the vigor, the greater the theoretical results. The accompanying chant was equally important, invoking the goddess of amplitude. *We must, we must, we must increase our bust,* said over and over again.

By the time I was a junior in high school (now living with my father and back in public school), mammary anxiety started to creep in. *What if I'm not a late bloomer and I'm merely destined to have the body of an 11-year-old?* Mired in convoluted teen angst, self-consciousness clouded otherwise carefree girly endeavors like wearing a swimsuit, workout clothes, or a prom dress. My kumquats were the tail wagging the dog undermining my entire sense of femininity and budding womanhood.

Fast-forward to college. I would be lying if I didn't admit that the insecurity about my darn boobs factored, albeit minimally, into my willingness to explore lesbianism. I didn't feel the pressure to have an idealistic body by male standards. You could say it was a perky bonus. In fact, my girlfriend was equally unendowed. It was she and a mutual friend who chartered the Itty Bitty Titty Committee with me. Fortunately, the perspective had shifted to light-hearted self-deprecation rather than the self-disdain that I had from high school.

My early-mid 20s ushered in a couple of notable changes. I now had a long term boyfriend (the one from the River Phoenix incident) and a steady career in the fitness industry. My chest was still flatter than Ben Stein's affect in *Ferris Bueller's Day Off* but I had a plan. I saved my money over the course of a year and bought myself some melons. And melons indeed they were. I had wanted oranges (C cup) but ended up with cantaloupes (DD) thanks to a rogue plastic surgeon with a mind of his own.

Hoisting those suckers around for many years was an infinitesimal price to pay for a supernumerary reward. I felt sexy, hot, and curvy and loved every damn minute of it—until that is, my boobs functioned according to their biological purpose. Lactating for three babies turned a pair of cantaloupes into a pair of watermelon torpedoes. Eventually, though I got my Goldilocks boobs that were just right (my Cs) after I was done donating my body toward the propagation of the human species. *¡Viva las tetas!*

Before we break out the maracas, I need to admit that there was a somber undertone below the surface of my chi chis.

The existential brooder within me called into question my higher self. *Rachel, are you really that vain that you require plastic surgery to feel good about yourself? You must be a superficial person. And think of all the hungry mouths of orphan children you could have fed with the money that you spent on those silicone bags of excess. What message are you sending to other women? That they can't accept their bodies as beautiful just as they are? You say you are a deep person but are you really? Fake boobs? I mean, c'mon girl. Where are your values?*

Clearly, my vanity was greater than my altruism.

Or was it?

The question of values is precisely the lynchpin issue when it comes to vices and vanities. My tale of two titties, and all the soul searching that went along with it, ultimately clarified two dominant values that have always and will always shape my life: Enjoy Life. Elevate the Lives of Others.

Growing up in a hyper-religious home steeped in southern culture invariably came with black and white thinking on nearly everything. As it pertains to human behavior and morality, there were explicit "do's and don'ts." You do listen to Christian radio. You don't listen to secular music. You do procreate because God commanded it (within a heterosexual marriage of course.) But you don't ever talk about sex or suggest that you enjoy it. You don't cuss. Even words like *crap* and *fart* are "bad." You never admit that you desire something material. (Hasn't the Lord provided everything you need?) You never eat the last piece of cake. (You're not worthy of it.) You never put much effort toward your outward appearance, lest you commit the sin of pride. *You don't drink, don't smoke, what do ya do?*

I was, in fact, a Goody Two Shoes. All of this evened out for me throughout my early adulthood, as I'm about to share with you now. But even before I understood my personal positions on these various topics fully, I had learned that I would not sacrifice exploring the many fun facets of being human.

Investing time and resources into what makes life fun and enjoyable for me can be equally yoked with deep conviction and compassion to help others. I would even argue that stoking both of those aspects of living fortifies each other. When I invest in my own enjoyment of life, I have more energy to give to others. And when I give to others, I find more enjoyment in life.

Starting as a young child I was always finding ways to help others. I used to ride my bike every morning, in the opposite direction of the school, to put the newspaper on the porch for a little old lady, named Mrs. Broom, who lived on a hill. I would initiate visits to a local nursing home and visit seniors. In college, I organized community events to serve local underprivileged children. And throughout my adulthood, I have consistently volunteered in many capacities to serve senior adults, disadvantaged children, the homeless, and other people in need. I've never done these things because I felt like it was a rote obligation. Rather, such service expanded my heart and I always have felt that I am the one who benefits.

I'm sure you've heard the expression, "Your strength can be your greatest weakness." While this is typically referencing an individual's proclivities and traits, I think this also applies to the whole of humanity. Vices and vanities are merely archetypal exaggerations of some of the best expressions of what it is to be a living, breathing, fully alive human.

Confessions

Confession #1: I'll Drink to That!

Alcohol has a weird history with Christianity. On one hand, it figures prominently in stories and traditions about Jesus. Jesus not only drank wine, but he is also said to have turned water into wine and instituted it as part of The Last Supper. On the other hand, Christianity was the basis for the Temperance movement in the early 20th century and some denominations, to this day, have strict policies against drinking.

I received similar mixed messages growing up. My grandmother proclaimed lifetime abstinence while my stepfather would have already downed several beers on his drive home from work every day. At dinner time, he would sit on the sofa with his TV tray watching sports and clap his hands together when he wanted more beer. That was his way of summoning me to bring him another Miller Lite.

When I had left crazy, Christian, cult-land to go live with my father in my junior year of high school, I maintained a healthy respect for the law and didn't drink at all until I was 21. I am grateful for those formative years because they fortified the pleasure of enjoying life on its own terms. Later, I definitely had my young adult drinking binges but they were infrequent and regular drinking was never a part of my lifestyle.

Years later after having been married to a man with severe, assorted chemical dependencies, I do not write about alcohol lightly. I have lived and witnessed the terrifying destruction that addiction causes a family. Alcoholics Anonymous calls it a "family disease" for a reason. This disease is purported to be caused by biochemical imbalances and/or personal loneliness and despair. Most recently, it is estimated that 1 in 8 Americans is an alcoholic, nearly doubling the statistic from the early 1990s.[xvi]

It would be a gross misappropriation for me to attempt to write about addiction with even the slightest hint of authority. The subject matter is too grave and my experience is limited to living with it, not studying it, particularly from a clinical perspective. For that reason, I want to acknowledge its existence and role in American life, defer to other professionals and experts who are attempting to cure its broad cultural permeation, and thereby limit my focus in this discussion about alcohol.

My chosen focus is the 7 out of 8 Americans who are not alcoholics but who navigate the pervasive presence of alcohol in our culture and daily lives. Is there such a thing as a balanced way to incorporate alcohol in our lives?[xvii] The short answer, as I see it, is you get out of it what you put *into you*.

If you drink every night, the calories add up, your biochemistry changes, and your clarity of mind may be altered. Motivation and productivity may be affected depending on how much you are drinking. Ultimately, it is a matter of evaluating your values and making behavior choices based on them.

On the other hand, I have found that I must allow for some "kick up the heels" kind of fun. Some of my happiest experiences are with my man drinking margaritas all day by the pool at our favorite spot in Mexico. Or having drinks with some girlfriends while we swap war stories. I know my boundaries and I own my choices.

Relentless self-examination over the years regarding alcohol (and other vices and vanities) have led me to crystallize some simple guidelines. They work for me and free me to balance responsibility with a lighthearted spirit.

Personal Mantra
I can have a crazy fun time with people I love and trust *and still be a deeply spiritual person*. I refuse to ascribe to an unattainable, puritanical ideal that those two aspects of being human are mutually exclusive.

Instinctive Pull
The unceasing drive for humans to alter their consciousness through alcohol or other chemicals points to our inherent need to transcend our "monkey minds," releasing the noise between our ears. In and of itself, this *need* is understandable, necessary even, for our happiness and contentment. The *method* though should be chosen wisely.

The Caution
The concern is that we shouldn't artificially rely on external agents to transcend our misery and find our happiness. This is like trying to grasp a vapor between your fingers. This also can bring us dangerously close to or being consumed by addiction, which is toxic for all people. Meanwhile, abstinence is unrealistic for most people. We must embrace the hard work of managing the tension in between.

The Takeaway
Vices begin and end with personal accountability.

Confession #2: Sex, Sex, Sex

The greatest irony about sex is this:

When you're in your 20s and still have your youthful, hot body, you are insecure and have no idea what a healthy, meaningful relationship is about. By the time you mature (we hope!), knowing who you are and what you expect in a partner, you are circling your 40s and your body is in the early stages of various rebellions. And if you are a woman and have chosen to have babies, then your body has been to hell and back.

Ok, maybe that's not you—just me.

Sex in my 20s was quite literally feeling my way around in the dark. I had no idea what it was supposed to be about. So, sex was more like a performance. Something that you had to act out. It doesn't mean that I didn't genuinely care for or love the people with whom I had relationships. But my own sense of self and understanding of love was quite limited at the time, thereby making sex a shadow of what it is capable of being.

Sex in my 40s...? Um, I'm blushing here. Let's just say it's been like entering a 5th dimension, a reality that I never previously knew existed. My life partner devotedly loves me despite my foibles and midlife body. I do not need to be perfect for him but his love for me inspires me to be all that I possibly can for him. There is exquisite beauty in our ability to *see* one another as full-range humans and love each other in our entirety. This dynamic fosters mind-blowing sex.

Sex suffers from polarization in our culture just like so many other facets of westernized humanity today (politics, economics, religion, to name a few). On one hand, there is the commercial-ization of sex in such forms as copious pornography, strip clubs, and virtual reality experiences, and to a subtler degree, the saturation of media messaging that sexualizes women and men in order to sell things. Unrealistic expectations are benchmarked about women's bodies, what women truly desire about sexuality, and what men should demand from women. These manifestations of sexuality are like cotton candy—lots of fluff, temporarily satisfying, but ultimately empty calories that will make you sick if you partake too much. Typically men are the consumers and women are the pawns in these scenarios.

On the other hand, there are fantasies of a different nature that are sold to women, in which they are the consumers and men are the pawns. These fairytales don't immediately deal with sex but are the foreplay, so to speak, for sexual and romantic expectations of women. They go something like this:

Your one true love is out there, waiting just for you, you princess, you.

Your man intuitively knows how to make you happy. It is his obligation to make you happy.

Your man should put you on a pedestal, with fawning adulation, pacifying your every emotional need.

You will ride off into the sunset for the rest of your life with your hero prince.

Whether women manufacture these fantasies themselves or they are sold to us by "Hollywood" or "the media," they originate from a kernel of truth about cisgender womankind. Despite the bold dialogue and advertisements for vibrators these days, I hold firm that what most women really want, more than an out-of-this-world orgasm, is *romance*. Sex is bonus territory. However, placing misguided and unrealistic expectations on the nature of men is not fair to men or women.

Both ends of this sexual continuum have merits. There is truth in the raw, naked force of sheer sexual energy that undergirds male fantasies. Sex is, after all, the biological impetus for life itself. And the female fantasies are buoyed by the inherent need for emotional connection, which makes life deeply fulfilling and worth living.

It is the exploitation of either of these polar ends that causes problems. When we have a false reality established about the opposite gender, we limit our ability to have authentic con-nections, dwarfing sex to a hollow experience. This is no less than a form of deflecting reality about ourselves and other people. The fundamental commonality between men and women, regarding sexuality, is that they desire *to be desired* (not to be confused with lust). I think most people admit that they know the difference between "sex" and being fully desired. The former is mechanical and often transactional in some way (you do this, then I do that). The latter is an inexplicable convergence of sexual energy that produces a unified consciousness.

The drive behind the desire to be desired is the need for Love. We want to be *seen* and loved for the entirety of who we are. There is no greater vulnerability than quite literally being naked with someone else. Sex is a conduit for Love when all is aligned in a healthy way.

However, it is not the responsibility of one person to complete the heart void of another. When we know Love within ourselves and honor it in others, we no longer expect another human to fulfill our deepest needs. This paradoxically, in turn, frees us to have the most intimate sexual and emotional connection with our partner.

Personal Mantra
I can dress like a stripper for my man if I want to. We can swing from the chandeliers if we want to. *And I am still a deeply spiritual person.*

Instinctive Pull
Humans crave to return to our origins—the power of Life. Sex is exactly that.

Caution
Escapism.

The Takeaway
A vice that leads to personal escapism disconnects us from ourselves and others.

Confession #3: #@$%!!! Yeah!!

Hell yeah, I cuss. And let's be honest, so do you and most people you know. In fact, the power of curse words is diminishing because the practice has become so common. Words that once were considered so taboo that they would never be uttered in polite society are now being slung around like patties on a grill by the mouths of teen YouTube stars, celebrities, and politicians. It seems nearly anything goes these days.

Except maybe in one arena. Church.

In my last few years as an Adult Sunday School teacher at "Hilltop Methodist," I occasionally tested the boundaries and would drop the word *shit* in a conversational lesson. I think most people thought nothing of it, a few people actually appreciated the real talk, and only once did a couple get up and immediately leave. My intention was to close the gap on the double standard of "proper" behavior at church and real life outside of church. I think the vast majority of Americans are tired of double standards, period.

What are curse words anyway? Merriam-Webster says they are a "profane or obscene oath or word." Digging more deeply, *profane* is characterized by irreverence or contempt for God or sacred principles and *obscene* means offensive to morality or decency, repulsive.

According to that definition, modern American evangelical Christianity curses more than all the raunchiest stand-up comedians combined. It may sometimes be offensive when vulgar language demeans people or natural acts (like bitch for women and the F word for sex) depending on context. But in my estimation, that is a first-generation offense. At least the typical use of these words is transparent and honest with their intention.

Consider this...

Have you ever had a sanctimonious Christian say to you, perhaps with a pat on your hand, "I will pray for you" and your inside voice wanted to say out loud, "Please don't."

Have you ever seen zealous preachers quip about Jesus, Jesus, Jesus being the only way to salvation... and your reward is coming after you mail in that $50 check?

Have you ever been physically beaten in the name of God?

I've experienced all of those things (and much more), and I'm sure you can relate in theory if not in personal experience. What is happening in these types of scenarios is that key words like *pray, Jesus,* and *God* are being used in perversive, disingenuous ways by people, knowingly or unknowingly, who have selfish, egotistical motives and ambitions.

In the above three examples, it is the subtext of superiority, greed, or violence that corrupts and bastardizes words that, in their pure form, should evoke peace, inspiration, and Love. It is like offering someone a chocolate cupcake that *looks* like a chocolate cupcake but is made out of dog poop, all the while insisting that it is delicious and fulfilling. At least when most people use traditional curse words it's their way of saying, "Here's a piece-of-shit cupcake. Enjoy!"

Not only have these words been co-opted by errant, self-seeking religious folks but the concepts that the words represent have been too. I think this is why it has become so popular for Americans to say, "The Universe is telling me to do this or that" or "The Universe gifted me this or that" because the word God has become offensive to so many people. I even contemplated whether I wanted to use the word God in this book for that very reason.

As our concept of God evolves, as I am advocating in this book, abuse of these sacred principles are commensurately offensive to morality and decency. The rise of the Nones reflects the repulsion of these defamed words, such as God, that are used to promote hatred, bigotry, exclusion, hypocrisy, and arrogance.

There is no greater profanity than defaming the concept of Ultimate Love while using the word God! Alignment of the mind, heart, and mouth reflect authentic living.

Personal Mantra
Clean heart, (occasional) dirty mouth.

Intrinsic Pull
Humans seek to verbalize the full range of our perceptions of being.

The Caution
Words matter but it is the heart, mind, and intentions of words that can impart actual damage.

The Takeaway
Vices, like words, have the power, intent, and application that we give them.

Confession #4: Music is Family

Music is a universal language. This cliché has resounding favor with people who optimistically want to see humanity get along like the famous Coke commercial of the 1970s. There are detractors of this aspirational platitude too, primarily citing that music is a reflection of both particular cultural contexts and physics based on musical structure and related instruments.

It may not surprise you by now for me to say that I think music is both a universal language and dependent upon context. Which is exactly what the human race is like. We are One yet have different expressions within our oneness.

What is interesting to me about music is how territorial and judgmental some people can be about their musical tastes versus that of other people. Facebook feeds are a sportive playground to watch this play out. Some friends make fun of how commercialized and diluted pop artists are, claiming that only indie artists have anything genuine to say through their music. I have a few Facebook friends who are diehard metalheads and scoff at softer forms of the art. Supposedly if you really love classical music, you are a nerd. Country music is stereotyped as being for simple people. And there is the perennial disdain of rap by many white folks that teeters on yet another manifestation of racism.

I must explain the reason that I included music in the chapter on vices and vanities. In and of itself, music is neither. But generations of people have often *perceived* music as some sort of vice, particularly when it disrupts the status quo. I immediately think of the scandalous advent of rock and roll in the 1950s, or the female sexual liberation of Madonna in the early '80s, or the in-your-face cultural commentary of hip hop and rap crescendoing in the '90s. For those on the "outside" of these respective audiences, music was quite often viewed as something dirty or sinister.

Similarly, in contemporary times, we have a tendency to perceive music affiliated with groups of people other than our own as less legitimate, less enjoyable, and sometimes offensive.

One time while teaching an indoor cycle class several years ago, I played *Get Back* by Ludacris. It was the full throttle version complete with M'fers, which was entirely deemed acceptable in the club where I taught. About halfway through this song, my otherwise hardcore sweatin,' jamming class was interrupted by two women who brusquely got off their bikes and left. I had no idea why until one of them approached me after class.

She was a licensed psychotherapist and the other woman was the director of a local shelter for family violence victims. She proceeded to tell me that they simply could not tolerate any song that advocated violence, explaining their work in the domestic abuse realm. I heard her out, respecting her perspective and apologized for making them both uncomfortable. Since that time, my knowledge of their life's work to protect abused people has deepened my gratitude of them.

Here's the kicker though. Neither of those ladies knew that I myself had been a victim of domestic violence both as a child and as a former wife. They didn't know that I had feared for my life countless times and was still, at the time of this occasion, dealing with a threatening ex-husband. The song I played actually emboldened me to stand up to him and whenever I played that song, it rallied my strength *against my abuser*.

Later I scrutinized the lyrics to see what it was that they found so offensive. All I could detect was hyperbolic language about a guy who was telling another guy that was messing with him, to back the fuck down. Personally, I dig the shit out of that message.

My conclusion from that experience was that those women heard a few keywords, without knowing the full message of the song, within the genre of hip hop and derived their own derelict conclusions. The fascinating caveat to me is that I had played many other songs in different genres—dance, pop, disco—with far more exploitive, albeit gilded, language that went entirely unnoticed by these same women.[xviii]

Music reflects people. It can reveal the best of us and the worst of us. It can be particular to a subculture or universal in its appeal. But its essence is an expression of what it is to be human. I cannot possibly know what it is to grow up in South Central L.A. or experience the struggle of working-class farmers or feel the immense pressure of pop artists hamstrung by corporate contracts. But I do understand what it is like to face oppression, to struggle to make ends meet, and yearn to have free agency over your career. Behind the music is a universal expression of humanity.

I view all types of music as open letters to the world. Some individual pieces of work may be better composed than others or have a greater depth of meaning than others, but all of it is a reflection of what makes us human, for better or worse.

Personal Mantra
I may not like *all* music (just *most*) but I respect all peoples' rightful, authentic expression.

Intrinsic Pull
To connect with others.

The Caution
To shoot the messenger, the artist being the messenger.

The Takeaway
Vices and vanities are like music. They reflect and exemplify the good, the bad, and the ugly of human experience.

Confession #5: Food

You can live without alcohol, sex, a dirty mouth, or Ludacris, but you cannot live without food.

Food can become a vice for Americans perhaps much more easily than in most other parts of the world due to our relative affluence.[xix] We overeat to absolve unhappy emotions, gorge on highly processed, unhealthy foods, revel in super-sized meals, and want it all at cheap prices.

Frankly, this is kind of a toddler mindset. *I want what I want, when I want it, NOW. Mine, mine, mine.* Trust me. I know. You should see me during Girl Scout Cookie time.

Our national abundance is gloriously displayed on several cable food channels with programs that showcase the mastery and creativity of chefs and bakers, leaving viewers drooling. Commercial-grade kitchens with snazzy appliances and pantries equipped with vibrant fruits and vegetables and exotic ingredients are eye candy for those of us on the other side of the television screen.

Meanwhile, more than 12 million American children struggle with food insecurity, regularly being hungry. A widely held belief purports that this affects their performance in school and increases their likelihood to get into trouble. Further, low-income families are much more likely to offer poor quality food to their children because processed food has become more affordable than fresh, nutrient-rich food from natural sources. This, in turn, affects brain development. Along with other factors, the cycle of poverty grinds on.

How are we to understand this disparity and what are we to do about it?

It's really simple. If you have more than you need, build a longer table, not a higher fence.[xx] This can be done on an individual, micro basis by inviting people to your home for shared meals. It can be done through volunteering at local food banks or sharing food with the homeless. Or if you are so compelled, engaging in broader efforts to address hunger nationally or internationally.

I absolutely love cooking for others. For as long as I've been busy in the kitchen, I have shared food with people outside of my immediate family—some in need of a meal, some simply in need of comfort or company. Most recently, my youngest daughter and I have been supplying home-cooked meals for a local family violence community for women and children fleeing abuse. We bring homemade meals like Texas goulash, Louisiana gumbo, lasagna, or chicken noodle soup, providing a nourishing welcome for these courageous families on the first night of their new life. Those meals are cooked with Love and I hope they are fed as much by Love as they are by noodles or veggies!

Sex may initiate life but food *sustains* life. It is no wonder that religious traditions often center around food. As previously explored, Christian communion is modeled after The Last Supper. The Passover Seder is one of Judaism's most beloved rituals where families celebrate a traditional meal and recount family and religious stories. In Buddhism and Hinduism, prayer altars are adorned with fresh fruits as a means of offering back to the divine what has been given to humans—the very thing that maintains our life.

Food reminds us that the sacred is found in the ordinary. Our higher selves collapse into our biology through the practice of gratitude for our sustenance. We are reminded of our humble origin as a species yet celebrate our intangible connection during a shared meal. Bonds of joy and poignancy are formed when people gather together and break bread.

Personal Mantra
Share a meal, share Love.

Intrinsic Pull
To return to the humble state of gratitude for what is provided for our survival.

The Caution
That we take our sustenance for granted, with lack of appreciation.

The Takeaway
Share meals with people. Everyone will be better off.

Confession #6: Money

I've observed a curious thing about money during my lifetime. It doesn't matter how much you have or don't have, people judge each other using money as the barometer.

People with less money often judge people with lots of money as being greedy, power-hungry, or superficial—as if they all have an agenda to "take advantage of the little guy" and that wealthy people live in a problem-free world.

People with more money often judge people with little money as being lazy, dependent, and looking for handouts—as if they don't have a work ethic and that they bring their problems upon themselves.

I've known people with little money who are greedy and super-ficial. I've known wealthy people looking for handouts (college admissions scam ring a bell?). I've known people with little money who largely consider themselves to be problem-free. I've known wealthy people with little work ethic.

Human tendencies are human tendencies, regardless of economic status. The best and worst of us cuts all ways.

I once heard a preacher say, "How you spend your money and your time says everything about you." Of course, he was extolling this platitude within the context of prompting people to tithe to the church. Regardless of his motivation, this expression has always stuck with me. It's pretty darn true. It really doesn't matter how much money you have or don't have, what you do relative to it reveals much about who you are.

The piety of *"I don't need money"* works if you are a trust fund baby or genuinely are compelled to spend your life in the Peace Corps. But that is not the reality for most Americans who work hard and still struggle to get by. Let's drop the pretense that money doesn't matter. It matters. Anyone who says that they don't care about money is either lying or has never been without it. And while it doesn't buy you happiness, it sure can make life a lot more pleasant.

Money is like alcohol—how it affects you reflects deep parts of your inner nature. Money is like cussing—we use it to express ourselves for better or worse. Money is like sex—there are often complicated emotions, thoughts, and motivations behind how we understand it and how it works in our lives. Money is like music— throughout all of recorded human history, currencies have existed as universal means for transactional gains. Money is like food— realistically, we need it to survive in this world and if you have more than you need, your excess should be leveraged to help heal those in need.

Personal Mantra
Humbly receive. Humbly give.

Intrinsic Pull
To live out our values.

The Caution
Having purely selfish values reflected in the way we utilize money.

The Takeaway
Find the balance between enjoying what money can afford you and elevating the lives of others.

Confession #7: Image

Do you remember the story of me being rejected as a candidate for ordination in which I was later told that my sweater was too tight during the interview? That committee meeting took place on a Wednesday. Four days later on Sunday, I was scheduled to serve, as I always did at the time, on the chancel in church wearing an alb and rope.

I loved wearing an alb with the rope tied around my waist. It felt like an echo from the distant past when churches had humble means. The gauzy linen robe and the utilitarian belt evoked a humility all people should not only possess during church but during life.

But that particular Sunday, I was pissed. I had been judged and scorned because of my appearance and past traumatic life experiences. I had a lifetime of memories whereby the church, as an institution, wielded its power to diminish and penalize me— usually for transgressions that *someone at the church* committed toward me, no less.

I decided to make a statement that Sunday without saying a word. I wore bright red lipstick and bright red, sexy AF heels—with my alb and rope. Right there. In plain view for the entire congregation. On the chancel. Serving communion. Saying the Prayers of the People. Reading the Bible. Yes, churchy judgy people, if you are going to judge my heart because of my sweater, boob size, or the fact that I have endured abuse my entire life *from people within the Church,* then I might as well give you more to talk about.

And guess what? I am loved and I love *just as much* wearing my hooker heels and fuck-me lipstick.

The truth is, I was more my authentic self by wearing both the alb and the Jimmy Choos. I have always been a study of opposites when it comes to fashion and self-expression.

I love to pair designer heels with clothes from Target. There is something deeply rewarding to me about this clash of socio-economic fashion paradigms. I admire the creative minds of fashion designers who experiment with ways to both reflect our current societal values and chart where we're going.[xxi] I also appreciate everyday clothes at a good price. And, I buy used designer clothes because I value originality but not overspending.

I am a firm believer that "you wear the dress, the dress shouldn't wear you." The whole idea is that *you* are a gift to the world. How you present yourself should reflect your inner consciousness about who you are.

The greater kicker is, we can present differently at different times and *still* be authentic to who we are. Sometimes I wear sweatpants, a baggy t-shirt, and my hair in a floppy bun with no makeup *and I still know my power*. Sometimes I put on a pair of kick-ass heels with a form-fitting dress, ready to take on the world, *and I still know my vulnerability*. Sometimes I wear something super carnally sexy for my man, *and I still know I am a spiritual being*.

However, if I do not keep my awareness elevated, my thinking can devolve. Endlessly wearing sweats can reinforce a lackluster interior sense of self. Endlessly putting on the "power suit" can lead toward a maniacal frenzy about looking perfect or assuming the intense energy that often goes with it. I can't think of anything negative about being super sexy for your boo. Ok, well actually, if we are more concerned with *looking* sexy than *being* your own authentic sexy self, then there is a problem.

When we become attached to the exterior as a means to define our interior, rather than our interior defining our exterior, then incongruency of being occurs. This instigates ripple-effect problems, which can lead to the abuse of other vices and vanities.

It is worth noting that traditionally people categorize someone as vain if they put excessive effort into their outward appearance. Of course, what is excessive to one person is normative to another. So again, only an individual can draw that line for themselves.

However, a person who puts little to no effort in their outward appearance could also have fallen prey to vanity. How? Their outward appearance may be a reflection of their hollow understanding of themselves. Perhaps such a person needs to step into their personal power, which in turn would influence their self-care. Either extreme of excessive or deficient outward self-care may reflect a shallowness of the person's sense of self.[xxii]

The idea of presenting an external image of ourselves does not need to be rooted in sheer vanity, though. Rather, we can understand the genuine human desire to be the best version of ourselves. We should celebrate different individual styles as people explore who they are, expand their self-awareness, and prompt the rest of us to rethink assumptions and embrace diversity.

Personal Mantra
You do you and rock what you got.

Intrinsic Pull
To feel like the best versions of ourselves.

The Caution
That we attach our identities to our outward appearance at the expense of our inward consciousness.

The Takeaway
Congruency of being is when our awareness unites our interior and exterior presentations.

The Dovetail: Parting Thoughts, Summations, and a Send-Off

I'm Here for the Chicken Wings

I faced a hooters dilemma in my mid-20s. I was teaching countless fitness classes per week and practically lived in workout gear. While I always held myself to exceedingly high professional standards, I also joked that it was an unusual profession in which I was paid to get sweaty with groups of people half-naked.

The "crisis" I faced was that scores of people had seen me for years wearing sports bras and tights. And you may recall that my sports bra served little practical purpose because there was *very* little for it to cover. So when I decided to get a boob job, I had to figure out how I was going to address the sudden appearance of my new endowment.

It was easy actually. I told the truth. And humor didn't hurt.

You can't go from a size A- to DDs in a jog bra leading throngs of people through movement without potential awkwardness. So I took control of the narrative—I was expecting twins and my classes would get to meet them in a few weeks, wink wink, nudge nudge. I owned the reality, diffused murmuring and gossip, and then strutted my stuff after the twins arrived without shame and with joy!

On Hooters, Freedom, and Having It All

I would like to see us be honest about our vices and vanities. This would dispel the erroneous mystique that often clouds them in our corporate consciousness. With such honesty, the power of the vice or vanity is taken away from *it* and squared back within *you.*

Vices and vanities can come in a great variety of forms. I covered some of the classics. Additionally, the modern age expands our options for means of escape and self-indulgence. Some examples include drowning out the world by playing video games for 12 hours a day, overworking to avoid intimate relationships at home, compulsively buying stuff to fill a void, or projecting an artificial version of yourself on social media.

The question is, who or what is in control here?

Freedom is not only when we have the liberty to *do* something we want to do. Freedom is also having the inner fortitude to *not do* something we think we want to do. Paradoxically, this freedom is borne from a solid sense of self-awareness, accountability, and control.

Understanding ourselves in this way allows us to explore fun, expansive outlets of being human in a way that causes no harm to anyone. Within the perspective of the Greater Whole, this freedom should deepen our gratitude for life and thus our compassion for others. Our First World Responsibility should always ultimately override our own personal pleasures so that through Love, we help heal our One Human Family. And there is nothing wrong with having fun along the way! To me, this is the essence of living a deeply rich, exceedingly fulfilling life.

How's it Working for Ya?

I started this chapter regaling you with the story of my anterior proportions. There is no better way to see this theme through than with an homage to the Buxom Queen herself, the venerable Dolly Parton.

Having been born and raised "dirt poor" but surrounded by her family's love in the Smoky Mountains of Tennessee, Dolly catapulted to fame soon after high school as a songwriter, singer, and actress. She has captured the hearts and imaginations of Americans for over 50 years with her ample talents and um, attributes. She is the first one to find humor about herself, poking fun at her big, blonde wigs (one for every day of the year), her weight fluctuations (eats low-carb during the week and whatever she wants on the weekend), her famous breasts, her acrylic nails, and wearing makeup just in case there's an emergency and she has to leave the house. Dolly says of herself, "I may look fake but I'm real where it counts."

Dolly invested much of her wealth into her home community in East Tennessee when she built Dollywood, an amusement park that provides thousands of jobs and pumps money into the local economy. She is humble, quickly deflecting praise to others and recognizes spiritual discipline as integral to who she is. Countless people who have interviewed her or written about her attest to her genuine nature. All the effusive things you hear about Dolly and her kind, loving ways? Yeah, she's really like that—in real person, even when the public eye isn't looking.

I can only aspire to have many things in common with Dolly but there is one thing that I know for sure—we both love red lipstick and red heels. Whether or not you share our proclivity for those embellishments, let's try to be like Dolly in other ways. May we be honest about our indulgences. May we be generous with our abundance. May we be humble of heart, finding reasons for gratitude in all things. May we live a life of congruence, being the same person in the world that we are in private. And may we be grounded in Love.

It is now time to roll up our sleeves and get cracking on our last topic. Channeling Dolly's beloved anthem about being on the job 9-5, let's clock-in and see how Religion is working for us, as both individuals and a society.

CHAPTER 7

RELIGION

This was my final year to take ballet. Being forced to quit ballet was one of my greatest losses for many years. However, life carries on and there are always new adventures to be had!

Opener: The Great Toenail Exorcism

Have you ever been at the center of an ingrown toenail exorcism? Don't be jelly but I have!

I was a young preteen lying supine on the teal reclining sectional in our taupe living room that was adorned with mauve accents and faux floral arrangements. That '80s interior design nightmare may be enough to scare you but the truly frightening scene was taking place around my left big toe.

This was my third year as a student of ballet. It was my greatest joy. And in fifth grade, our little ballet troupe began pointe classes. This caused me to get ingrown toenails fairly regularly. My stepdad had determined this was nothing short of the devil's work. His theory about Satan was that if something went wrong in our bodies, it was because Satan was deliberately attacking us or we were sinful and allowed Satan to infiltrate us because we weren't living a holy life. Nevermind the fact that my adolescent feet were crammed into a pointed toe box and bore the entire weight of my body during practice.

Fortunately for me the theory in Toenail-gate was that Satan was attacking me and it was no fault of my own. So I escaped a beating but received an exorcism.

My mother pulled out the fancy olive oil from the bright yellow cabinet above the electric stove. It was fancy because the usual cooking oil was vegetable oil and olives are from the Holy Land, hence fancy. And since it was virgin, it was even holier and fancier.

My parents decided my toenail warranted the big guns.

For some reason, church people from out of town were always revered as being larger than life. As if they were extra spiritual, extra churchy, extra Jesusy. There happened to be another couple visiting in town who was from west Texas and part of this cult network. They were invited over for the great toenail exorcism in addition to a couple of other people who were the sheep to my stepdad's shepherd status.

I'm lying down and my mother unveils the olive oil from Piggly Wiggly like Harrison Ford presenting the Holy Grail. I am surrounded by men wearing Aqua Velva, women in shoulder pads and clownish eye makeup, and a Redneck in Chief with a god complex. My mother anoints me by making the sign of the cross in olive oil across my forehead. I remember thinking to myself, *Am I supposed to be feeling something after being anointed? Is something supposed to well up inside of me? And why not use a Crisco stick or sprinkle confetti on my head for that matter?* All of it seemed arbitrary.

Team Exorcist laid their hands on me from head to toe. My stepdad begins the invocation by emphatically reminding God how great He is. Everyone else reinforces the flattery by murmuring in hushed yet convicted tones things like, "Yes Lord," "Amen," and "Praise your name." My stepdad eventually turns his attention toward telling Satan what a sack of shit he is, at which time the peanut gallery shifts into an indignant tone, "You are the father of lies," and "You shall be overcome." (The use of Old English was a nice touch.)

I noticed there was an art to being part of the prayer backup singers because you didn't want to upstage the lead singer. So they had to be careful about using long phrases or being too loud. Otherwise, there would be sensory overload for God. And it might piss off my stepdad who had the floor.

Team Exorcist lathers themselves up. The fervor builds ultimately unleashing the pinnacle cacophony: speaking in tongues. If you are unfamiliar with this phenomenon, this is the curious practice of some Christians to hurl nonsensical sounds from their mouths in the belief that the Holy Spirit is speaking through them. Essentially it is God (Holy Spirit) praying to Himself using a language only he understands. (Insert thinking emoji face here.)

It sounds something like this:

EEEko labbuh labbuh sookemashi andale andale OHHH sokaymooo esobuhlay neeshohhh bippity boppity boo shiloh mo koi attuh praise you Jesus EEEko labbuh labbuh shama lama ding dong!

I was paralyzed in the eye of the storm while the circus swirled around me with escalating intensity.

Not only was my stepdad a religious ringleader, exorcist specialist, and a Southern Bell telephone repairman, he also performed small surgeries. After the power of God had been sufficiently summoned and the glossolalia had apexed and subsided to an empty calm, he pulls out some fingernail clippers and some rubbing alcohol.

He began digging around on the side of my toenail with the pointed file of the clippers. I garnered all my willpower not to recoil and shriek with pain. Had I done that, his Ego would have been wounded and I would have displayed an apparent lack of surrendering to the power of God. I had 12 hands laid about my body, Satan expelled, and the fear of God and nail clippers within me. I don't even remember if he removed the ingrown part of my toenail or not. I just remember bewilderment, confusion, and a holy ton of pain.

Eventually, Team Exorcist was satisfied with their work and dispersed. I think the foreplay was more exciting for them than the actual completion of spiritual intercourse. I limped back to my bedroom. Though I was only the tender age of eleven, I sure could have used that proverbial cigarette.

Menu and Music: Higher Mountains

Our menu thus far is bursting at the seams with Eclectic Salad, Carbs Schmarbs Bread, Believe in Love Veggies, Obsequious Pot Roast, and Lord Have Mercy Apple Pie. Topping it off is The Balancing Act aperitif.

What more could I offer you without being overwhelming? I don't care what Martha Stewart or Rachael Ray appear to do on television, preparing meals (and the cleanup that follows) takes wayyyy longer than a 30-minute cooking show.

So lest we make this meal more of a burden than the joy that it is supposed to be, the final menu item is not something that you will make to be consumed. Rather, it is something that you all *do*. For those who are willing, it is an opportunity to share of oneself with the group as an extension of gratitude and connectivity.

Check out the Recipe Appendix for the icebreaker that I call Roots.

Perhaps while you are setting your table, you'll enjoy the Queen of Soul, Ms. Aretha Franklin. In the meantime, I will wrap up my present journey with you with the fervor, optimism, and conviction that she had while belting out *Climbing Higher Mountains*. After all, at the end of the day, we're all just trying to find our home.

The Backstory: Can't Live With It, Can't Live Without It

Consciously or unconsciously, I think many American Nones are in a state of shock, much like I was at the conclusion of the Great Toenail Exorcism. We are orphaned by our religious heritage because it has become like an estranged family member who is no longer recognizable, defying our sense of rationality, justice, and civility. It is not so much that religion has changed. We have. But for the better. The fact that religion *hasn't* changed is precisely the problem.

I have woven throughout my credo (of sorts) personal tales fraught with religious abuse, misuse, and incredulity. Trust me, I have left a holy ton of material out of this narrative, only having given you the sizzle reel. In my final chapter of confessions, I am left to answer one overarching question.

As an American None, how am I to understand my relationship with religion now?

Let's start with the basics.

It should come as no surprise that scholars have debated the definition of religion for centuries, some limiting it to a manufacture of purely Westernized thought and others elevating it to supernatural, divine status, with endless other variations in between. It is a study in and of itself—philosophy of religion—to study the study of religion.

I must admit that I enjoy such philosophical mud wrestling, gratuitously slinging abstract dirt around with the erudite perception that the outcome actually matters. To be fair, philosophy is grossly underappreciated in our culture. This is because the mental heavy lifting of philosophers has a significant lag time in directly affecting everyday people. So with humble deference to philosophers of religion, I will redirect.

Let's keep it real. When you or I are talking about "religion," we have a pretty good mutual idea about what we are talking about, despite the impressive academic gyrations of PhDs who, like Bill Clinton, want to parse things like what the definition of *is* is.

Chances are, when you think of religion you are simply thinking of *a belief system that involves shared practices with a like-minded community, all centered around moralistic and supernatural claims.* Boom. Maybe I just spared you a degree in philosophy of religion. Ok, it can get far more complicated than that but for our purposes—real people living today in the real world—I think it is a solid start.

Take this conventional definition of religion and cross-reference it with what comes to mind when you think of what religion is. I would imagine you could *add* to my definition but fundamentally this definition should work. This skeletal framework should conjure categories like Christian, Muslim, Jewish, Hindu, etc. Or, even more specific subcategories like Episcopal, Suni, Hasidism, or Hare Krishna respectively.

I need to pause and ask you a very important question now.

Have you ever had classic Tex-Mex cuisine? The creamy, fake yellow cheese dip, aka queso, that coats your arteries with every scoop you consume from that salty, crispy tortilla chip? The requisite accompanying frozen margarita with just enough sweet and sour to counterbalance the chips and just enough tequila to make you think you look good dancing? The ooey gooey sour cream chicken enchiladas or fajitas loaded with guacamole and shredded cheddar? This is the kind of meal that will make you nap all afternoon—after they pry you from doing the Boot Scootin' Boogie on top of the bar.

There is one thing that both Texans and Mexicans can agree on. Tex-Mex cuisine is neither truly Texan nor Mexican. It has taken on a life of its own and folks just can't get enough of it.

This example of hybrid cuisine is similar to what happens with religion. Lines get blurred and it is often hard to tell where one influence ends and another begins. This is not a new phenomenon. Incipient Christianity itself is an amalgam of Jewish theology, Greek philosophy, and Roman culture, not to mention all the myriad local expressions unique to specific geographies as the religion spread around the globe. Celtic Christianity, Egyptian Coptic Christianity and innumerable syncretic forms of Christianity, if experienced separately, would almost seem like entirely different religions.

Like the seismic shifts of plate tectonics from hundreds of millions of years ago, religions and cultures have collided, merged, or blended sometimes violently, sometimes slowly throughout history. Things are different now, though. The world stage in the Information Age is accelerating *everything,* including the expansions and contractions of religion.

A few years ago, prior to adopting my None status, if you had asked me what my religious affiliation was, I would have said, "I am a Taoist Christian." But that was really short for being a Taoist-Buddhist-Jewish-Al-anon-Methodist-JesusLover-Christian."

My spiritual development has been greatly influenced by all of these thought-systems, and to lesser degrees many others. Their respective philosophies changed the way I understood spirituality in general and Christianity specifically.

For example, Taoism purports the balance of all things, working in harmony toward the goal of homeostasis. Whereas, Christianity is more oppositional (good vs. evil, heaven vs. hell, etc.) and conflictual with the belief that ultimately good will triumph over evil. Buddhism teaches that acceptance of things as they are is central to inner peace. Christianity teaches that there is always hope beyond your current situation and prompts you to long for a better day. The Talmudic tradition in Judaism taught me that it is ok to question existential claims and not have all the answers. Al-anon made spirituality simple, practical, and non-judgmental. Methodism extols the notion of Grace.

At the risk of oversimplification, I found that these Eastern and Western thought systems fundamentally reflect different orientations to understanding ultimate reality. Yet, the more deeply you study these disciplines, particularly in their mystical traditions, it becomes evident that Eastern philosophy is implicit in Western religious thought and vice versa.

This was an illuminating epiphany for me during the dark years after my second divorce. In that marriage, I had been on the Christian treadmill doggedly putting one foot in front of the other, shoulders slumped, head hung low, just praying and praying, "believing" that God would change my life for the better. I was in my late 30s and my hope was running out. I felt like a sucky Christian because I wasn't happy and I didn't see any promises being delivered.

It wasn't until I was going through my divorce and studying Buddhism again that the key to my happiness was unlocked. I learned how to accept life on its own terms and find happiness in the present. Yet Christianity worked to help me maintain a long-distance vision for a changed life in the future. I resonate both with the Happy Buddha and with the triumphant message of Jesus' resurrection story. They equally played a part in melding a holistic spiritual message that I needed to hear and implement in my life.

The shrinking of our planet due to a digitally connected world is hastening both the spiritual and practical needs of people to glean more holistic spiritual truths. I have seen this play out many times during Adult Sunday School at Hilltop Methodist. I often taught about Jesus from the mystical Christian perspective, which I found to be very much in line with Taoist and Buddhist philosophy.[xxiii] People's eyes would light up when I told them that resurrection was a concept that they should be experiencing today—it's not about the afterlife. Or when I empowered them to identify the divinity within themselves, in the hope that they would then be free to see it in everyone. There is a *hunger* for complete spiritual messaging.[xxiv]

The subject of spirituality and religion has consumed my entire life. Despite my forlorn experiences with it, religion is the only readily available vehicle that even attempted to teach me wisdom about existential matters. I did not learn about Love through the study of algebra or sadly, even much from my family. I was not taught forgiveness through my years as a working adult in the business world. I did not understand my totality as a human, being both of a divine and fallible nature, by being a participant in civic life. Religion was the portal that unlocked the wisdom behind these facets of being that applies to all aspects of life.

I have examined religion as one would when considering the purchase of a used car. Looking under the hood, turning dials, revving the motor, flipping switches, running it idle, and taking it on multiple test drives. Religion may be flawed and in need of an overhaul but like an old jalopy, it will keep honking and backfiring and driving us nuts if we don't upgrade it. And I maintain that as a species, we still need it to get around.

In the remainder of this chapter I seek to lay out my perspective, in effect calling for a peace treaty between religious and non-religious folks with the ultimate aim of focusing on what unites us, not divides us, as One Human Family. While religion, in its present form, does not work for me and many millions of other American Nones, we have the power, if rooted in Love, to reshape how we think about religion and how it functions in our society.

Confessions

Confession #1: Religion is Inevitable

People frequently complain that they have a problem with *organized* religion. In our country and culture, the person saying this is usually of Christian heritage. (This is just a numbers game because our country is primarily of Christian heritage. However, I have met people of many other faith backgrounds who share this view.) The contempt ranges from casual disregard of religion to outright outrage at its very existence.

I find this interesting for two primary reasons. Firstly, in the simplest definition of the term, Christianity is anything but organized. Depending on your source, there are roughly 1500 different denominations and sects in the United States alone and this does not include the countless, "one-off" independent churches. Plus, within each of these groups, there are differences of opinions and interpretations of beliefs, doctrines, and practices. The Christianity Family Tree makes a Jerry Springer family reunion easy to understand.

Secondly, in the abstract sense of the word, it is the nature of humans to organize. We categorize concepts and systems so that we can better navigate a world that would otherwise come hurtling at us in a seemingly capricious, cannibalistic way. Have you ever heard anyone bemoan the existence of politics, the economy, or the educational system, for example? Yes, we may have beef with aspects of these societal spheres, maybe even calling for reform, but we don't resent the fact that *as an organized construct* they exist. They are necessary for the functioning and efficiency of our society.

So it is for religion.

I think what people really mean when they say they have a problem with organized religion is that they have a problem with *institutionalized* religion. To help clarify this point, consider this. Politics, the economy, and the educational system are not in and of themselves institutions. They are social structures based on societal needs. Within each construct, various definitive institutions may exist, but the overarching *concept* is not institutional.

Institutions take on a life of their own and far too often fall prey to abusing their power. While abuse of power exists in the realms of politics, the economy, and the like, there is a key differentiator with religion. As a human-made mechanism, religion makes ultimate, existential claims that strike at our deepest concerns: to love and be loved and to have a sense of place and purpose. Our Egos sometimes mistakenly think that we can satiate these needs through political, economic, or academic gains. Meanwhile, religion claims to have *THE* answer when everything else inevitably falls short of absolving our discontentment or unhappiness in life.

And that's why people are disenchanted—because the promises aren't delivered. This is similar to the point that I made about curse words in the previous chapter. The defamation or misuse of concepts (exemplified in the form of words or religious institutions) that are by definition meant to heal and spread Love are exponentially more offensive to people than the misuse of other concepts that don't make such audacious claims. It speaks to our bone-marrow deep, existential human ache and commensurate expectations of religion that millions of Americans are now divorcing themselves from it. The hurt and pain are that profound.

The pronouncement that religion is inevitable should not be confused with the notion that I am advocating that all people *need* religion. I am simply saying that religion, as a societal construct will always exist. After all, there is no other societal construct that seeks to do on a broad scale what religion does—satiate our deepest existential needs. So we might as well make peace with it. But there is some serious work to be done before we'll all be holding hands and singing *Kumbaya*.

Confession #2: The Finger Pointing to the Moon

In Chapter 1, I explored how God is a metaphor for our deepest needs as humans and how words themselves are metaphors for our perceptions and experiences. In Confession #1 of this chapter, I explained how religion, like politics or economics, is a necessary, organized human social structure stemming from inherent needs. I also identified one key differentiator between it and other social structures—that religion makes bold claims about our ultimate existence, which is why people are soundly rejecting religion due to its failure to deliver on such promises.

There is one other key distinction between religion and other social constructs. Taking politics again as an example, it is a *transactional* construct with *tangible* benefits or losses. At least in American democracy, we vote for politicians because they are supposed to perform certain tasks—hence, the transaction. This practice yields taxes or no taxes, improved highways (or not), federal programs to feed the hungry (or not), legislation to expand or curb human rights, etc.

Religion, on the other hand, is an *unconditional* construct and firstly and foremostly has *intangible* benefits or losses. Modern American Christianity, particularly Protestantism, extols these ideas. According to them, by the grace of God, a person is able to freely receive God's gift of salvation. Freely equals unconditional and salvation equals intangible. Yes, there are expectations of beliefs and behaviors in order to remain in the Christian fold, but the price of admission is free and the ultimate reward intangible. (In theory.)

This "unconditional, intangible" premise sets itself apart from all other human social structures and arenas. Thus religion, as a social structure, is also a metaphor. It is an elaborate exercise, replete with ornamental doctrines, practices, traditions, and history that, when deflated from such embellishments and when informed and guided by Love not Fear, seeks to transform a person from pain into joy and darkness into light.

Bruce Lee channels a common illustration used in the Buddhist and Hindu religions to explain this idea. In *Enter the Dragon,* he says to a misguided student who is too caught up in his head, "It is like a finger pointing a way to the moon. Don't concentrate on the finger or you will miss all that heavenly glory." Now unlike Bruce Lee in this clip, I wouldn't whack you on the head but I do share his perspective.

Where religion has gone abysmally wrong throughout history is when individuals or groups of people are focused on the finger at the expense of experiencing the cosmic awe beyond it.

Confession #3: We Are All Healing from Something

During my second marriage and for a time afterward, I frequently attended Al-anon meetings. Al-anon is the companion program to Alcoholics Anonymous, designed for anyone who has a friend or family member who has a problem with alcohol. Like any 12-step program, traditionally people introduce themselves by their name followed by "...and I'm grateful to be here" or something along those lines. But there was another slightly acerbic identification that often followed a person's name. It went like this:

Hi, I'm Doretha and I'm a recovering Baptist.

Hi, I'm Walter and I'm a recovering Catholic.
Hi, I'm Sam and I'm a recovering Jew.
Hi, I'm Ryan and I'm a recovering Hindu.
Hi, I'm Cindy and I'm a recovering Unitarian.

You get the drift. And then everyone would wax on about how their religious system of origin caused them irreparable harm all these years later. But here's the really fun twist. The Baptist had converted to Catholicism. The Jew had converted to Unitarian Universalism. The Hindu had converted to being a Baptist. And so on. It was like a shell game where everybody just swapped out each other's religions, all in the attempt to find the hidden truth somewhere. If only one could select the right coconut!

People convert from one religion to another because the new model doesn't possess the baggage of their religious heritage or associated previous life experience. Sometimes people are successful with a new religion because its particular emphases or community happen to match their particular needs or deficiencies. A different religion seems fresh and not laden with disappoint-ment. It's kind of like when a kid won't eat broccoli when his mom makes it but when he's at his friend's house, he thinks Timmy's mom's broccoli is the bomb.

After making this observation over many years both in Al-anon and out in the world, I had an epiphany.

We are all healing from something and religion in and of itself is not the problem. (Nor, in and of itself, is it the solution.)

The problem is Soylent Green. Oops, I mean, *people*.

I suppose to be fair, living on this planet can cause its own challenges independent of human agency. Famine, tsunamis, shark attacks, and mosquitoes come to mind. But the truth is, how we humans handle life and one another is the root issue. Institutionalized religion, after all, is made of *people*.

With the understanding in mind that religion is a necessary human construct, a means not an end, and that human beings shoulder the culpability for most everything that ails us, I will escalate our discussion to address one question. *What are we to do with this knowledge?*

You can religion swap (like I used to observe in Al-anon meetings) or you can religion drop like the 90+ million American Nones. But at the end of the day, what we all need is the simple, comprehensive truth of Love lived out amongst each other.

Confession #4: Two Rights Don't Make a Wrong

Once we are liberated to recognize religion as a means but not the end (finger not the moon), then we are free to respect different "truths" espoused by different religious or non-religious folks alike.

Let's take what-happens-to-us-after-death for example. A Baptist may believe that they will be greeted at the pearly gates, reuniting with mom and pop, Aunt Ethel, and Buster their dog from second grade. A Catholic may be worried about being snared in purgatory for some long forgotten, unconfessed sin. A Jewish person may believe that they will live on in a place called Sheol, joined by the deceased righteous of any people or faith. An atheist may believe that we return to the dust and that's that, thank you very much. And as for this American None? I am content knowing that my body will perish and hope to leave a legacy of Love that will live on through the people my life has affected.

These varying positions on the afterlife are the respective truths for those who hold them. While some people get all sanctimoniously critical about such beliefs, I just want to ask, "Who really cares?" Meaning, if so-and-so believes you sprout wings after you die and play golden harps while floating in clouds, what is that to you?

I don't believe that Jesus literally rose from the dead but I don't have a problem with people who do. If a family adheres to strict kosher laws, more power to ya! If going to confession every day helps keep your heart light, confess on, brothers and sisters!

My point is, for American Nones who are skeptical of institutionalized religion, please be mindful that for many adherents, these beliefs and practices provide a deep sense of meaning in their lives. If a person's life is grounded in and lived out by Love, then their personal religious beliefs or practices should be of no concern to others. Likewise, religious folks should not be obsessed with those of us who do not share their doctrinal beliefs.

When I was in seminary, my most beloved professor was an Irish evangelical, the only self-professed evangelical on faculty. He and I immediately recognized that we respectively represented vastly different theological orientations. As you have read, my primary issue in modern, American religion is how evangelical Protestantism has misused and abused its position in our country, marrying tribalism with dogma. So how is it that the professor whom I admired most was evangelical?

His theology was far more conservative than my progressive leanings but he was one of the most humble, loving people I've ever known. He respected the differences of others, having no agenda to manipulate or change them. His way of evangelizing was to serve destitute people, with a particular ministry in Romania. We may have disagreed on the doctrine of the Trinity or the virgin birth of Jesus, but we were united on the role of God as Love in the world.[xxv]

I have no doubt he quietly thought that I was off the mark with my suppositions on many things. Yet, he encouraged me to explore and find my own theological way saying in his Irish lilt, "Ms. Roberts, if you're going to be a liberal, be a good one!" He was telling me to do my due diligence and be thoughtful about any assertions I may make. I always felt unconditionally accepted by him despite our gravitational differences.

I learned from this academic relationship and the years of volunteer work within an urban interfaith organization, that the power of Love unites people despite radically different religious or non-religious doctrinal beliefs. It is only when dogma is not undergirded by Love that beliefs can create abysmal ripple-effect problems. Like I said in Chapter Three, firstly and foremostly, we must believe in Love. The rest takes care of itself.

The Fullness of Love Experience

A profound sense of loneliness has followed me around most of my life, having never felt rooted by my family of origin nor by a home base. Friends have always been a select few here or there despite having innumerable social and professional acquaintances. As a result, I would unfairly place the demand of filling my deepest ache for Love on my romantic partner du jour. It was a subconscious choice but nonetheless one that I made. That is a horrible thing to do to another person.

Paradoxically, it took losing two marriages, feeling disenfranchised from the Church, being largely disconnected from my family, having no close friends at the time, and being unemployed to discover Love. I felt stripped of everything that had previously defined me. There was absolutely nothing that could distract me from myself.

First I had decided to ward off the beast within me. I shared this with you in Chapter 5, The Plano Experience. This is where I banished Pain from my being once and for all. If there is such a thing as exorcism, that was it. Not an actual demon, but a venomous energy vanished like a vampire flees light.

Second, I had to shed a faulty construct of God. I shared this with you in Chapter 1, The Rosedale Experience. This awakening allowed me to *see* Love as God, rather than the human artifices we attribute to God. In banishing Pain and subsequently a false God, an empty space was created that needed to be filled.

Enter Love.

Here's how it went down.

After I had left my second marriage, it became irrefutable that my schtick of trying to be the perfect wife or Christian did not produce peace or joy or guarantee favorable outcomes in life. There is no medal awarded to martyrs. The question became, *What was **my** role in my perpetual unhappiness and toxic situations in life?* After all, it takes two to tango.

This is when the real essence of Love illuminated my consciousness. Revelations of sacred truths unfurled that foundationally changed me.

My deficiency was *not* standing in my strength—the strength that originates from Love. This sounds simple but in reality, it packs a profound punch. Humans have confused Love with myriad things:

servile obedience, controlling tactics, indifference— it runs the gamut. In this particular scenario of mine, Husband #2's "strength" (in the form of dominance) was not from Love. Neither was my sparkly wifey behavior and resentful compliance.

I had been buying into a faulty understanding of Love my entire life (which was intimately intertwined with my old conception of God). I finally understood what I needed to do to change myself and not repeat old patterns.

Rise, Rachel, Rise.

Rise to the fullness of who you were created to be. Rise to the fullness of Love.

In having a Right View of self, I recognized the stark state of my anemic being. *This* was a healthy form of humility. In this space, I understood that anything Good about me is not *of* me but is from Love. I was everything and nothing at the same time.

For the *very* first time in my life, I knew that I was Loved just by being alive. I am valuable simply for being part of the Greater Whole. I am part of a Story that is vastly bigger than my own life. Life flows through me, it does not happen *to* me. Like a dawning of ultimate awareness, a sense of exhilarating freedom unleashed.

Within that freedom, I found my place and purpose.

My place is being part of the bigger Story. My purpose is being an instrument of Love. In the letting go of trying to orchestrate the appearance and machinations of my individual life, I saw my Oneness with the divine majesty of everything both mundane and transcendent about the world that we know. The Fullness of Love flooded me like a dam that had been waiting for decades to burst.

Through the lens of Love, I realized that all of the people and institutions who had previously hurt me had fundamentally operated from their own Pain and Fear. My stepfather, the cult, my parents, Husband #2, Megachurchland... any and everyone. Love liberated me to compassionately see all of them as products of our total human condition. I realized that anyone who is operating from Pain is really coming from a deep place of being desperate for Love.

The clincher enlightenment was that I am essentially no different than them. I know what it is to be desperate for Love and to act on Fear. My personal dysfunction may have manifested differently but the essential commonality remains. Understanding that I was neither greater than, nor less than other people brought Love full-circle.

This life-altering epiphany made it instantly illogical to hold anyone or anything responsible for my lack of Peace or Joy. Love was right here, right now for my taking. I saw clearly that every single person whom I have ever encountered has been prey to inherited dysfunction and has authored their own mistakes—*just like me*. It is fruitless to trace unhappiness to other people because they themselves could just point down the human chain to someone else. It would never end. How far back must we go to find the source of our misery when the antidote is within us and always has been?

This in turn, allowed for forgiveness, which ultimately is a cosmic untethering from being energetically beholden to Pain. Forgiveness does not mean one merely looks the other way and remains in unhealthy interpersonal dynamics or toxic relationships. But it does mean that they are not a slave to the past, do not have the mindset of a victim, and *do* allow the other person the liberty to come into their own fullness, with or without them.

Many humans grasp onto our individual lives like trying to capture a fistful of sand from the stream of an hourglass. This is based on the illusion that the universe centers around us for the span of the several decades that we are alive. We do not own Life but we are responsible for owning our choices while we participate in it.

The most fundamental choice that any of us ever make is whether we live in Love or Fear. When we choose Love, purely from the desire to be in union with it, then our lives reap exponential rewards. Perspectives change. Positive energy attracts positive energy. Love begets Love, and Peace and Joy follow suit. Love transforms us from living death to Fully Living.

The death of Pain and the birth of Love is nothing short of a resurrection story.

Confession #5: Moving the Goal Posts

We can all rejoice that the slaughter of goats, throwing babies in volcanoes, and marrying off twelve-year-old girls are no longer socially acceptable forms of religious practice. The history of religion, spanning continents and cultures, is ripe with many more examples of (what now seem like) wackadoo beliefs and practices.

As human consciousness evolves, we collectively find acts of violence and bigotry intolerable, especially in the name of religion. Fear of those who are different from us subsumes into the knowledge that all humans are fundamentally the same. Advancements in science eclipse antiquated explanations for natural phenomena previously explained by myth and super-stition. Nones and people from progressive religious orientations understand this.

It is time for Nones and religious progressives alike to raise the bar for what is acceptable within the functionality of religion. Nones must be willing to work *outside* of religion toward this aim. Meanwhile, religious progressives can work *within* their religious organizations to shift the mentalities and behaviors of their ilk. Both will further positive change for the whole of humanity.

There are three primary areas where expectations should be reset within religion—the cessation of bigotry and oppression, general education about the history of religion, and the role of science over supernatural claims.

Firstly, it should be unilaterally understood that the interpretation of religious texts or traditions is no longer justification for the mistreatment and abuse of people or the earth. Whether it is based on gender, sexual orientation, race, disability, age, or any of the other host of reasons that one group may seek to diminish another group, it must stop. Period. Any oppressive religious edicts still existing should be understood as part of an antiquated people's journey on this planet. But living today, we (should) know more and can do better, which brings me to the second issue.

Americans are woefully undereducated about religion. I'm referring to it both as a societal construct *and* significant religious events in the historical timeline.

The average Christian knows very little about the objective history of their own faith, much less anything credible about other world religions. For example, knowing that epic floods (like Noah's) and virgin birth myths existed in ancient pagan cults that far predate Christianity puts the biblical claim of infallibility in perspective. Many American Christians are entirely ignorant about other branches on the family tree like Ethiopian or Orthodox Christianity that have ancient roots. All they know is the theatrical, prosperity gospel of our times that has become conflated with capitalism. Such knowledge right-sizes the notion that there is only one way to be a Christian, which extrapolates to the truth that there are many legitimate ways to be human. Christians need to study the history of their tradition from outside, non-biased sources generated from academic research and studies.

Conversely, non-religious people could shore up their knowledge but from the opposite angle. At the offset, it is not unusual for atheists and agnostics to be far more knowledgeable about the history of Christianity, and to a lesser extent, other religions. In part, this is because they are fed up with the misuse and abuse of religion, so they are more motivated to point out its flaws. However, as someone who has the equivalent of nearly two master's degrees in theology and *still* walked away as a None, I observe a gaping hole in the knowledge base of many fervent non-religious people.

There is a lack of understanding of what has worked *well* via religion and how it can still serve a constructive purpose in our culture if handled responsibly. Embedded in much of the archaic doctrines, superstitious stories, and unscientific claims, are existential truths that ancient peoples discovered about love, forgiveness, trust, acceptance, peace, harmony, and many other redeeming facets of life.

Additionally, much of our health care, educational, political, and humanitarian infrastructures have religious origins. Further, while those in power frequently misused religion throughout history for selfish gain (and many still do!), the vast majority of *believers* were (and still are) ordinary people yearning for meaning in their lives and connection to something greater than themselves. One must respect the spirit of that.

Lastly, Nones and religious progressives must advocate for the primacy of science over supernatural claims. It doesn't matter to most Nones if someone else believes Jesus literally rose from the dead or that crystals cure cancer. Until that is, it matters. Supernatural claims are fine for individuals to believe, but it becomes a slippery slope when collectively it affects other people and the greater good. Religions have a history of being discriminatory. The laws of science do not.

The coronavirus pandemic is a prime example of this. When factions of the country think they don't need to adhere to public health precautions because Jesus will heal them or the rapture is coming, we are all exposed to higher risk. When it comes to public policy, the facts of science must take precedence over supernatural worldviews so that we can do right by one another. Science needs to do its job while allowing religion to be a metaphor for plumbing the depths of the human soul.

This balanced view will help unify our One Human Family. And while we work toward this aim, we can celebrate the fact that gone are the days of passing snakes and burning "witches."

Confession #6: Redefining What It Means to Be Religious (Or Live Meaningfully)

At the beginning of this chapter, I provided this conventional definition of religion: *Religion is a belief system that involves shared practices with a like-minded community, all centered around moralistic and supernatural claims.*

This works for the classic understanding of religion—as a noun, a thing, a construction. But *to be religious,* as an adjectival state of being, carries a further nuance. This paramount distinction in how we understand ourselves as humans illuminates how we are all in this-thing-called-life together.

The nuance of *being religious*:
To be religious is an outpouring of oneself into a system of thought or behavior that is centered around *the human drive to discover a sense of place and purpose.*

Ultimately, this is really the base aim of conventional religion too. People want to belong to something and feel valuable.   These are core human impulses irrespective of any classification we give ourselves: socioeconomic, gender, race, creed, etc.

Christians, for example, may ultimately derive this through their religious faith. But I would argue that atheist mathematicians seek to find their sense of place and purpose in the abstract elegance and structure of math. Or that astrophysicists find their sense of place and purpose in their field of study, even if the net result to them is that we, as humans, are but specks of insignificant dust in the vacuous enormity of the universe. At least they have found "the answer" that they seek.

The word "religion" and its derivatives have become loaded in recent history. So for people who decidedly reject conventional religion, they may prefer the term "meaningful living" over "being religious," even if the latter is meant in the benign sense. In essence though, we are saying the same thing.

This nuanced understanding of what it is *to be religious* (or live meaningfully) also explains the practices of many Nones today who consider themselves "spiritual but not religious." They are rejecting conventional religion (noun) but are religious (adjective) in the way that they are devoted to their workouts and fitness communities, or their philanthropic work, or regular gatherings of friends and family over shared meals. Other examples include caring for animals, making or experiencing music and art, and exploring nature. A sense of place and purpose takes root in these and many other expressions of meaningful living.

Broadening the net with the definition as being *that where we find our sense of place and purpose* fundamentally gathers us together. This allows for a broad spectrum of expressions and unifies our One Human Family in spirit. We then see and respect each other's individual existential longings and journeys toward wholeness.

Confession #7: Be a Lover Not a Hater

There is only one scenario in which I ever feel emboldened to denounce someone else's spiritual or religious expression: If the product of that person's life, as informed by their faith, is based on Fear and propagates hate, division, and exclusivity. This, of course, applies to groups of people, too.

I know, I know. This position is a slippery slope and can land us into judgmental territory, which is precisely one of the chief reasons we are Nones after all. We certainly don't want to return judgy behavior for judgy behavior.

But sometimes the most loving thing a person, or society, can do is speak the truth. The power of genuine, life-affirming Love only grows when tended in a bed of truth.

Throughout my life, I have watched people try to grapple with the sinister underbelly of religion in our culture. This typically happens one of two ways. Either someone becomes what they disdain about the abuse of religion by being arrogant and spiteful themselves *or* they simply shut up and never talk about it, as if it is wrong to make critical observations about religion. Both of these approaches lend themselves to enabling some abhorrent religious practices. If you are extreme in your views, such as the former position, then you foster equal and opposite extremism because religious folks get defensive. If you just clam up, your apathy renders an open field for the further misuse of religion.

It doesn't have to be like that.

We *must* call out hatred, bigotry, and oppression. But we must evaluate ourselves and our own motives and tactics *before* we criticize others. Regardless of religious identification or lack thereof, we must come from a place of Love. It is the only thing that will save us from ourselves.

The Dovetail: Parting Thoughts, Summations and a Send-Off

A Reinvention Story

William Curtice was really onto something with his invention of the Creamery Swing Churn in the 1880s. Hailing from the humble origins of Eminence, Kentucky, Curtice offered the nation a more efficient method to produce creamy butter for their desirous taste buds. A large wooden container was suspended by a metal frame whereby a woman (because it was woman's work) would swing the churn rather than hand churn it like models of antiquity. Even more impressive was the foot pedal attachment that allowed a woman to rock her baby *while churning butter simultaneously*. Receiving a gift like that for Christmas must have been the equivalent of a husband buying his wife a powered vacuum cleaner in the 1950s. Merry Christmas, baby!

Another person who gained from this was a man named J. Fred whose woodworking shop manufactured these churns in Kentucky. He was a first-generation American and inherited the woodshop from his German immigrant father. He built a steady business making porch columns, stair railings, shutters, and the like for his local community. But J. Fred thought he had really hit the jackpot when he became an exclusive manufacturer of the Creamery Swing Churn. How modern! How cutting edge! The demand was sure to sustain a vital income for him and his family.

Much to J. Fred's consternation, his teenage son Bud threw him a curveball in his vision for the future. Bud, who had been apprenticing with his father, played hooky from work one day at the age of 17. He went to go watch a sporting event and came back eager to make sports equipment. His father derided this as foolish for nearly a decade. Bud eventually won out and J. Fred sold him the family business. Bud not only reinvented the company's purpose, he revolutionized a sport.

The company? Hillerich & Bradsby.

The sport? Baseball.

The product? The Louisville Slugger.

I don't know about you but I don't play baseball, yet I have known about the legendary Louisville Slugger my whole life. It's been such a commercial success that the moniker stands for more than just the bat. It is an *idea*, an ethos, something larger than life that can take on any adversity with might and tenacity—and *win*.

I'm also guessing, that like me, you have never churned butter in your life.

Bud, I think you hit a grand slam.

On Baseball Bats and Love

John A. "Bud" Hillerich transformed his family's business from a model based on (soon-to-be) obsolescent technology (butter churn) to a paradigm of thought leadership and production in the emergent sport that became "America's favorite pastime."[xxvi] His company led the charge in customizing bats per the specifications of professional players and advancing production methods that yielded better performance on the field. It was also his company that first introduced professional athlete product endorsements as a marketing tool, leading the way for the Michael Jordan/Nike-type partnerships of the future.

In this book, I am calling for a similar transformation of religion. We need to shed what is outmoded and non-viable and embrace the reality of the present and the future. Religious and non-religious people alike stand to benefit if we can be honest about what religion is and how it functions, finding our commonality in the *why* behind the *what*. Differences of doctrines, practices, and world-views need not be divisive if we are all motivated by what unites us: Love. It is time to redefine this social construct so that it can benefit our country and the world, not harm it.

Religion is like a baseball bat. You can use it to hit a home run or you can bludgeon someone to death. Many have chosen to drop the bat or not pick it up in the first place. Regardless of what one chooses to do or not do with the bat, the clincher is we, as individuals and as collective groups, *choose*.

Therein lies our freedom. In not blaming others for our woes, we release our power to choose Love. In changing ourselves in this way, we contribute mightily in transforming the world while discovering deep fulfillment.

The miracle in my life is not that I discovered Love. Rather, Love woke me from an existential coma despite all the human-initiated obstacles in its way. Therein lies the true miracle. Love works and proves itself greater than the abuse done in its name.

Now if you're like me, you may be frustrated thinking these sound like flowery, intangible words. Love schmove, you may be thinking. It's an overused four letter word. What does it mean in boots-on-the-ground terms? I get it. I've been there.

Diving into the simple but not-always-easy-to-do, practical under-standing of what Love is, and how to apply it in your life is worthy of a (future) tome itself. Where the rubber meets the road is where the action is, truly the only place that really matters.

So until we meet again, I hope it will suffice to leave you with a few thoughts on Love.

Love is greater.

Love is greater than brokenness.
Love is greater than Pain.
Love is greater than Fear.

Love dissolves confusion.
Love reveals clarity.

Love sees the other in oneself.
Love sees oneself in the other.

Love compels to speak truth.
Love stands firm in the face of adversity.

Love enjoins to build community.
Love gathers together.

Love lifts, empowers, and propels.

Love binds us, heals us, renews us.
Love is greater... than me, than you.

Love is Life.

The One in None

In the words of Sister Sledge, *we are family.*

You are my family. I am yours. There is One family—the Human Family.

I Love my family.

POSTSCRIPT

Ok, I realize my breakup letter may have caught you by surprise. Now, I've had some time to think through things.

You see, you are just not right for me in an intimate relationship kind of way. We can still respect and appreciate one another for our own uniqueness, though. And we probably have more in common than not. After all, we're all just trying to get by on this planet.

I'll take responsibility for my own stuff and you can take responsibility for yours. Let's focus on the positive and doing good by one another.

We can still be friends.

APPENDIX

Recipes

This is the super fun part! I love, love cooking and love even more sharing with others. Over the years of juggling the realities of life with my desire to create soul-satisfying meals, I hit my stride with a particular approach to cooking.

In a nutshell, it's the path of least resistance. This means, get the greatest benefit for the least amount of effort. I discovered ways to balance my love for the *process* of preparing food with the finished *product*. Here are a couple of examples. In my aperitif recipe I call for the use of honey rather than instructing you to make your own simple syrup. (Seriously, who has time for that?) And for the apple pie, I use a packaged pie crust instead of making my own from scratch. (The latter will surely test your strength of character.)

You will notice that I include shortcuts that allow you to enjoy the creation process without being overwhelmed so that you can get to the best part—sharing your meal with others and watching the joy on their faces!

This menu is a fall-inspired selection, intentionally meant to parallel the message of this book. We are living in a season where we must see what is old.

Simple, meaningful spirituality is most often found in the experience of the ordinary. Preparing meals to share is one of the best exercises for expanding our hearts and spreading Love in the world. Bon Appetit!

Lord Have Mercy Apple Pie

Whenever I say *Lord have mercy* I mean it like an epitomic Southern mama who is bewailing that her children tracked mud on the kitchen floor after she just mopped it. Or in my case, like a woman who occasionally resigns to the fact that sometimes you just have to eat the damn pie. The Borg were nasty buggers but they were right about one thing—resistance is futile.

This recipe makes two pies. That way you can either invite more people over for dinner or share one with someone who needs some TLC. You may want to purchase disposable aluminum pie plates at the grocery store for easy pie-sharing.

What you need:
- 10-12 medium or 5-6 ginormous apples
  - My favorites to use are a combo of Granny Smith with at least one of the following: Honeycrisp, Braeburn, or Envy
  - Peeled, cored, and cut into small chunks or slices depending on your preference
- ¾ c. white sugar
- 2 tsp cinnamon
  - I prefer Penzey's Ceylon
- ½ tsp nutmeg
  - I use a nutmeg grinder because I'm a cooking nerd
- 2 two-finger pinches of salt
  - (your thumb technically isn't a finger)
- 1 tsp lemon juice
- 4 tbsp flour
- 2 packages Pillsbury pie crust
  - The refrigerated kind that comes rolled up
  - (Unless you like a little self-flagellation, store bought is the way to go.)
- Silicone pie crust protector

What you do:
Preheat the oven to 400 degrees. Take the rolls of pie crust out of the boxes to let them come to room temperature before you unroll them.

Mix the apples, sugar, cinnamon, nutmeg, salt and lemon juice. Fold in a little love. (You know you have it to give.) Next, sift the flour over the apple mixture in 2-3 batches, stirring in between each addition. This fine dusting of flour will help prevent the pie filling from being runny.

Line ungreased pie pans with the pie crust dough. Make sure it lays down flat and evenly. Use a fork and make several pricks along the sides and bottom of each pan. Pour the apple mixture into both pans, dividing equally. Unroll the two remaining pie dough discs and lay across the top of the pies.

Unless you are Martha Stewart or her culinary progeny (in which case you will meticulously flute the edges of the pie crust), gently press the bottom and top pie crusts together around the edge of the pan. You can try to do something fancy or just let it be. Regardless, it's all going to end up in someone's belly.

Trim the excess crust off around the edges of the pie plate. Now imagine the happy faces of those who will eat your pie as you make a cut out on top of the pie to let steam escape. (Slits, shapes, whatever strikes your fancy.) You can also use the excess dough to make a design to put on top of the pie. I like to make my kids' initials.

Bake at 400 degrees for approximately 50 minutes until the crust is golden brown and the apples are fully cooked. After the edges of the pie are browned to your satisfaction (about 15-20 minutes in), put a silicone pie crust protector over it to prevent over-browning.

When the pie is done baking, remove and let cool on a wire rack for at least 2 hours. If you are making this pie for a dinner party, I recommend making it the day before.

Optional: Serve with *Get Behind Me Satan Caramel* (recipe is on the American None blog) and your favorite vanilla bean ice cream.

Eclectic Salad

The whole idea of *Eclectic Salad* is to experience a diversity of tastes and textures delivered via a cohesive palate. It is also meant to be a somewhat spontaneous creation, allowing you to use whatever you may have on hand in your kitchen. Be creative. The list below are merely suggestions to get you on your way.

I love this approach to salads because it mirrors life. We should celebrate all of our differences and honor what unifies us. Chomp on, brothers and sisters!

Salad Bed Pick one. Or more.	**Nuts n Bolts** Recommend 2-3.	**Sumpin Sweet** Pick one. Or more.	**Sumpin Salty** Pick one. Or more.	**Flair** 1 from each category.
Leafy green lettuce Romaine hearts Kale (see tip below) Baby Spinach Raw broccoli ribbons Shredded cauliflower	Grape tomatoes Cucumber Celery Sugar snap peas Carrot Green onions Avocado Boiled Egg Onion (a personal no-no)	Dried cranberries Grapes, halved Sun dried tomatoes Blueberries Strawberries Apples	Pumpkin seeds Marcona almonds Walnuts Pecans Macadamia nuts Pine nuts Olives Capers Pickled veggies or relish	**Cheese:** Parmesan Feta Goat cheese Baby mozzarella **Crunch Factor:** Nuts (see salty options) French's Fried Onions Snap Pea Crisps

Rinse and dry your leaf of choice for your salad bed. I use a salad spinner. Super useful.

If using kale, trim the tough spine from the leaves, chop into bite sized pieces and toss in a little olive oil. Massage the oil into the leaves and let sit while you prep your other ingredients. This will tenderize the kale leaves, making them more enjoyable to eat.

Pick your accompanying ingredients and slice, chop, dice, or keep whole depending on your preference. I recommend toasting your nuts. It brings out the full flavor. Then chop them to make them easier to consume. If your nuts are salted, I do not recommend selecting another salty ingredient such as the pickled items.

Toss the salad with your favorite dressing shortly before dinner time. A favorite go-to dressing recipe is as simple as combining 2 parts vinegar (balsamic, rose, or apple cider) to 1 part olive oil, salt and pepper. And if you prefer a sweeter dressing, add 1-2 tablespoons of honey. I shake my ingredients up in a closed mason jar before pouring. If there is any left over, it is already in a storable container.

Boom. Over and out.

Believe in Love Veggies

The inclusion of a veggie dish for this meal may seem redundant. After all *Obsequious Pot Roast* includes veggies and there is a salad on tap. This dish is either for the overachiever cook who wants to *do it all* or for your vegetarian friends who may attend your dinner party.

Vegetables are one of the things that I am most grateful for. They harness the life force of the earth in their nutrients, vitamins, fiber, vibrant colors, and unique tastes. Rather than disguise their complex beauty with sauces, I prefer veggie dishes that allow the star ingredients to shine on their own accord. (Just like you do!)

So whether you make this dish for your dinner party or save it for another occasion, the force is within you! Always.

Believe in Love Veggies is a fall inspired dish but you can substitute spring veggies if you prefer. Adjust the amounts of the veggies used based on your dinner party size.

What you need:
- 1 small rutabaga
  - Peeled and cubed
- 2 cups French green beans
  - Trimmed and cut into 2" segments
- 1 package sliced mushrooms
  - I love baby bellas
- 2 cups Butternut squash
  - Peeled and cubed
  - Trader Joe's sells this pre-packaged
- 1 medium onion
  - Halved and sliced
- 3 Mississippi drizzle of Udo's Oil
  - Olive oil works too
- Herbs de Provence
  - I prefer mine w lavender
- Ground pepper
- Freshly Grated Parmesan cheese
- Salted, roasted pumpkin seeds
- Chopped flat leaf Italian parsley for garnish

What to do:

In a large pot, bring 2 inches of water to a boil. Add the rutabaga, green beans, mushrooms, butternut squash, and onions. Lightly salt the water and veggies. Put a lid on the pot and cook for 5-8 minutes until all veggies are tender. The veggies should retain their vibrant colors.

Drain the veggies. Put in an oven proof dish. Drizzle with oil and fold in the herbs de provence and ground pepper to your liking. You can place, covered, in a warm oven (200-250 degrees) until ready to serve. Right before serving, add the parmesan cheese, pumpkin seeds, and parsley. Toss until evenly distributed.

Even folks who don't like their veggies love *Believe in Love Veggies.* Ask my kids! They will attest.

This was after my second divorce while I was finishing my master's degree. The children and I often rode our bikes to church. Soliciting their cooperation was like Armageddon. See how thrilled my son looks? Photo taken at Hilltop Methodist after I had served on the chancel.

Carbs Schmarbs Bread

Carbs. You can't live with 'em. You can't live without 'em. If you care about being healthy, you will only make this bread on a special occasion. Frequent refined carbs—no bueno. But everyone needs to kick up their heels once in a while. This simple recipe yields 2 domes of bread. Both can be used for your dinner party or you can share the extra fresh loaf with a neighbor. All who receive will be overjoyed!

What you need:
- 1.33 cup warm water
  - Straight from the faucet is just fine
- 2.66 tbsp cooking oil
  - Canola, Veggie, etc. I've even used olive oil in a pinch
- 2 tbsp honey
- 1.33 tsp sea salt
- 4 cups bread flour
  - All-purpose flour will work if that's all you have
- 2 tsp yeast
  - Bread machine yeast is preferable
- Bread Machine

Oh yeah... about *that*. Sorry for the bait and switch but I do recommend a bread machine. Well worth the investment. I bought an *Oster* for under $50 ten years ago and it is still alive and kicking. This is an example of maximizing output for less effort. You'll see how.

What to do:

Make the Dough
Firstly, begin the making of your bread about 3 hours prior to serving your meal. Work time is only 15 minutes. The rest of the time the dough is either rising or baking.

Put your bread machine on the Dough Setting. Make sure the paddle is in the bread pan.

Add the water, cooking oil, honey and salt to the bread pan. Stir. Scoop the flour into the pan. Hollow out a divot in the middle of the flour and place the yeast there.

Press the Start button. The machine will begin mixing the ingredients. Within the first 5 minutes, I scrape the sides to make sure that all the ingredients get evenly incorporated. After that, shut the lid and let the machine do its thing.

Chillax or Sumpin'

My dough setting takes a little less than an hour and a half. During this time, you can be preparing other parts of your meal, setting your table or taking a bubble bath. Whatever floats your boat.

Knead

When your bread machine alerts you that the cycle is complete, it is time to remove the dough for a final round of kneading and rising. Dump the dough on a lightly floured, smooth surface. The dough will be somewhat sticky. Using a serrated bread knife, gently slice the dough in half.

Knead the dough by folding it in half, starting closest to you and folding away from you while pressing *into and across* the dough. After one fold, rotate the dough ¼ turn and repeat. You will be removing air bubbles. Continue this method several times to allow the dough to contract and reincorporate with itself.

Meditate and Breathe

This is the sublime part of making bread. Just as the dough is folding into itself and recalibrating, allow yourself an interior journey of your own. Do you have hurts, worries, or disappointments that you need to release? Wherever you find yourself, imagine the force of Love working through you, filling you with lightness and clarity. With each fold of the bread, intentionally release what burdens you.

Inhale while you rotate the dough, exhale as you fold it away from you. Let your thoughts parallel this. Inhale as you think of your burdens, exhale as you release them, reminding yourself that you are ok right here, right now. You are enough, just as you are.

Let It Rest and Rise

Form the dough into two rounds, ensuring the seams are on the bottom. Place the domes on a lightly greased baking sheet a few inches apart so that when they rise and bake, the two shall *not* become one! Put a lightweight cotton towel over the bread. Let it rise for about 20 minutes or until doubled in size. The length of time depends on the ambient temperature.

Find your rest in the knowledge that you are Loved and you are Love. And, you will RISE out of, away from whatever pulls you down and into, toward the Life that propels you upward!

Bake and Let Go

Preheat oven to 400 degrees. Bake 15-20 minutes until golden brown. You will know it is thoroughly baked when you thump the top and it sounds hollow.

As your bread bakes, consciously remind yourself that *you* are not the things that seek to weigh you down. Align your identity in Love. Detach from Fear and Pain. May your resolve be as complete as the baking of your bread. It is a done deal.

Break Bread with Others

When your bread is finished baking, I recommend putting it in a wooden bowl lined with a cotton towel. Cover the bread with the towel to keep warm. You can slice with a serrated knife or literally break the bread with your hands as you pass around the table.

Serve with butter and honey.

Relish the communion of a shared meal.

Obsequious Pot Roast

The word obsequious and I have a funny past. We go way back—to the days in my 20s when I sucked at parties. I had read the word many times, alone at night in my apartment in various books and had even looked it up in my trusted paperback dictionary where I highlighted all kinds of new word discoveries. But what I didn't do was pay attention to how it was pronounced. I had just assumed it was pronounced:

obsie-QUEE-shush

Say it outloud. It's hilarious.

My annunciation was right-sized while on a date with a lawyer once. He tried to tell me how to pronounce the word and I proceeded to argue with him. He was gracious enough to let me think that I just might be right. Of course, the first thing I did when I got home was rush to my dictionary (this was the olden days, folks—1990s). The lawyer ended up being right about *obsequious* and other things—we weren't meant to be together. At least we had a good belly laugh before we broke up.

So why would I name this recipe *Obsequious Pot Roast?* Mostly because it makes me laugh. And if you mispronounce it like I originally did, it's even funnier. But I also chose this title because the secondary meaning of the word is "servilely compliant" or "obedient, dutiful." This serves as a reminder that all animals are at our mercy. When we consume them, I find powerful meaning in being mindful of that and our responsibility to be good stewards of life.

What you need:

- 4 lb beef chuck roast, salted and peppered on both sides
- Sea salt
- Ground pepper
- 2 tbsp olive oil
- 2 tbsp butter
- 1 32 oz. container of high quality beef broth
  - I love Trader Joe's
- ½ celery bunch
  - Washed, cut off both ends of stalks

- ◦ Keep the leafy parts
- ◦ Cut celery into 3-4 inch sticks, cut lengthwise if needed
- 1 lb carrots
  - ◦ Washed, peeled, & cut in 3-4 inch sticks, then cut lengthwise
  - ◦ My kids love the carrots so I add even more
- 1 large onion, diced
- 1-2 lbs of small red potatoes
  - ◦ Washed and cut in halves
  - ◦ I personally go light on the potatoes due to the starch
- 4-6 garlic cloves, minced
- 1 bay leaf
- 1-2 sprigs of fresh rosemary
- 2-3 sprigs of fresh thyme
  - ◦ (1 tbsp dried Italian herb blend can be used in lieu of fresh herbs)
- 3 Mississippi counts of Worcestershire sauce
- 3 Mississippi counts of soy sauce
  - ◦ (Yes friends, just count out loud—1 Mississippi, 2 Mississippi, 3 Mississippi—while you shake some flavor into your broth.)
- Chopped fresh italian flat leaf parsley for garnish

What you do:

Heat your dutch oven on medium-high until the pot is hot to the touch. Add the olive oil and butter. Allow the oils to heat up. After your moment of intentional gratitude for the beef, brown that wedge of glory by letting it sizzle in the hot oils, about 5-7 minutes per side. Don't be afraid if it gets over browned. Everything will be ok.

Remove the roast from your pot and add the veggies, herbs, half of the broth, and Worcestershire and soy sauces. Stir. Place the roast back in the pot, arranging some of the veggies to come up around the sides of the roast. The broth should cover the veggies but only come up halfway on the beef. Add more broth if needed.

Put the lid on the pot. Give it a few minutes for the internal temperature of the pot to increase. You may hear a slight boil from inside. Then lower the burner to medium-low heat. Leave that sucker alone for 2 and a half hours.

You will be tempted to open the pot before it's time. Halt thyself.

When the time has come, remove the lid and check to see if the meat is tender. It should easily pull apart with a fork and knife. If for some reason it's not, then cook a bit longer.

You can further season the broth if desired. My family eats Obsequious Pot Roast in a bowl and likes it brothy. Personally I prefer to pick out the potatoes and pour the roast and broth over a bed of steamed brown rice. Garnish with the parsley.

The Balancing Act Aperitif

Take a bottle of good bourbon. Pour 2 ounces over a block of ice. Swirl. Drink. It's that simple.

Ok, ok, ok. So you want something elevated?

What you need:
- 2 ounces kick butt bourbon
- ¾ ounce orange juice, fresh squeezed if you want to be extra
- 3 Mississippi squirt of local honey
- 1 2-finger pinch of ground Ceylon cinnamon
- 2 sprigs of rosemary
  - 1 for muddling, 1 for garnish
- Cinnamon stick for garnish, optional
- Ice

What you do:
In a cocktail shaker, combine bourbon, orange juice, honey, ground cinnamon, one sprig of cinnamon and some ice. Shake vigorously. This will effectively muddle the rosemary and release its flavor. It will also get the drink really cold.

Extra tip: Heat the honey for about 15 seconds in your microwave. It will thin the honey and make it easier to blend with the drink.

Use a strainer to pour into a small glass. I prefer small mason jars. Garnish with the second rosemary sprig and a cinnamon stick. Serve with a smile!

Admittedly, this is a shortcut version of making a curated cocktail. So if you prefer to muddle the official way or peel oranges to create a colorful garnish, go forth stalwart soldiers. But if you are a run of the mill person like me and are just trying to keep all the irons in the fire for your dinner guests, you may require my expeditious approach.

The Mocktail
In lieu of the bourbon, use your favorite apple juice and increase the amount to 4 ounces. Add 1 tablespoon Braggs Apple Cider vinegar. (Trust me on this.) Follow the rest of the recipe as is. Top with a splash of soda water for a little extra punch.

Roots—An Ice Breaker/Connection Maker

Go deep to grow up.

That's the idea of Roots. Hearkening the illustration of the Aspen root system used in Chapter 2, digging down unveils what unites us, which in turn energizes us to bloom.

There are three easy steps in Roots.
1. The host picks a theme.
2. Each guest writes down their response.
3. Before the meal begins, guests read their responses.

The theme can be something simple and broad like "gratitude," "blessings," or "reflections." Or perhaps something more invigorating and provocative like "what I wish were different about the world right now and what I'm doing about it," or "where the light has shone through my wounds," or "the funniest thing you'd never guess about me." Another option is to select a news story or cultural phenomenon of the week and pose a question around it for the theme. Or choose a movie or popular song that may instigate differing interpretations and commentaries.

Obviously the tenor of the theme should reflect the receptivity of the guests expected. I find that open ended questions work best and prompts people to give more robust answers. For more examples of themes, visit the American None community online.

The host can execute this fun ice breaker with unlimited creativity. A couple of suggestions include using a large glass jar, writing the theme on the outside of the jar using an oil-based marker, and having pieces of paper and pens readily available. Everyone can drop their paper in the jar and then before dinner, guests draw and read aloud someone else's response, allowing the group to guess who it belongs to.

Or, draw a big outline of a tree on a large sheet of paper or on a chalkboard. Write the theme on the trunk of the tree. Guests can sign their names on the roots and write their responses along the branches of the tree. There are also readymade "Gratitude Trees" in both 3D and 2D models available on the internet that provide a perfect application for Roots.

More importantly than exactly *how* Roots is delivered, connecting with others over a shared meal sows more Love in the world. And there is no such thing as too much Love.

ENDNOTES

ⁱ Studies from different organizations report different findings. The percentage of Americans who are Nones range from 23% (GSS, 2018) to 25% (PRRI, 2015) to 26% (Pew, 2019) to 34% (AFS, 2017). Based on today's estimated American population, these figures suggest that there are between 76 to 112.5 million Nones in our country.

ⁱi Buddhism doesn't actually purport a God. However, my studies revealed to me that the Buddhist notion of Ultimate Reality and the mystical Christian God were essentially the same thing. I'm sure there are many who would want to dispute this. But this was my reality and it ultimately freed me.

ⁱⁱⁱ I would find out years later that River himself grew up in a cult— The Children of God— that made my childhood cult pale in comparison. Fundamentally, both cults operated on many of the same tenets but Children of God is notoriously known to be a child sex slave cult. Something frankly, I think our organization could have evolved to had it not disbanded in the late '80s. Today, Children of God exists under the name The Family International.

^{iv}https://www.valuewalk.com/2017/03/scientific-explanation-human-mind-daniel-siegel/

^v The organization of my thoughts is based on what has worked for me to navigate life. You may observe an echo to Maslow's hierarchy of needs. His work and my present thesis are addressing different problems, albeit with some overlap.

^{vi} Matthew 7:3

^{vii} https://www.nationalforests.org/blog/tree-profile-aspen-so-much-more-than-a-tree

^{viii} John Calvin, the founder of Presbyterianism, is well known for espousing worm theology.

^{ix} "Right View" is a term borrowed from Buddhism, which in its simplest form means to see things as they really are free from personal biases.

^x This cult network was called The Shepherding Movement. Several books have been written by other survivors that go into greater detail about this insidious organization.

^{xi} The subject of homosexuality is directly or indirectly addressed in different books of the Bible, all written with different historical and cultural contexts. The face value position in all examples are not favorable to homosexuality at all. Strikingly, for an issue that has become a lightning rod for Evangelicals, Jesus himself had zero, zip, zilch to say on the matter.

^{xii} There are actually thousands of Christian groups who claim the Bible and their particular interpretation of it as their authority and justification for themselves. I'm just oversimplifying it for the sake of illustration.

^{xiii} The joke is, What does a lesbian bring on the second date? Answer: a U-Haul. This of course is a stereotype but from personal experience and observation, has origins in a bit of truth. I personally think it is because women are so relational by nature so if you pair two of them together, the chance of rapid coupling doubles.

^{xiv} Technically the euphemism "the family" referred to gay men, but I knew it to be an expression to refer to the gay community at large, lesbians included.

[xv] *The least of these* is a phrase lifted from Matthew 25:40. It is common Christian parlance used to refer to people in great need.

[xvi] https://www.washingtonpost.com/news/wonk/wp/2017/08/11/study-one-in-eight-american-adults-are-alcoholics/?utm_term=.defef3a63f98

[xvii] Sidebar note: According to recent studies, marijuana use is rapidly set to eclipse alcohol consumption for millennials. Pick your poison, I guess.

[xviii] Check out https://www.stuff.co.nz/entertainment/music/68067391/null for a list of *seemingly* innocuous songs.

[xix] Eating disorders are not part of the purview for discussion at present. I want to acknowledge their existence for anyone who may struggle in this way. These are complicated, grave matters whose sufferers deserve our deepest compassion.

[xx] Another one of my favorite internet memes.

[xxi] The link to The Devil Wears Prada is one of my favorite scenes in this movie. The irrepressible Meryl Streep channels an Anna Wintour-like character and schools Anne Hathaway's character on the value and influence of the fashion industry.

[xxii] Please note that I say *"may* reflect a shallowness."

[xxiii] The Gospel of John is considered to be the mystical book out of the four gospels and is a favorite throughout history for Christian mystics.

[xxiv] Even the current Marie Kondo craze about sparking joy through getting rid of clutter is inspired by her Shinto religious heritage.

[xxv] So as not to misrepresent my beloved professor, I must clarify that my characterization of Love as God would be considered egregiously defective to him. He maintained a more complex, traditional God as independent agent/deity. Where I leave off with God as Love, he would have considered just the beginning.

[xxvi] Yes, I know, football probably outranks baseball today. But as far as American lore goes, history will always reflect apple pie and baseball!

www.ingramcontent.com/pod-product-compliance
Lightning Source LLC
Chambersburg PA
CBHW061819040426
42447CB00012B/2727